The Lean Six Sigma Improvement Journey – Introduction

This book provides a map and guide for the ongoing improvement of existing processes. It lays the foundations to achieve Six Sigma performance, but it's likely you'll need some appropriate training to help you.

The method is supported by a range of tools and techniques, with high-level descriptions and summaries to help you. In the text these are matched to the most appropriate step. The tool-set includes a selection of Lean Thinking tools, as well as the more traditional Six Sigma techniques.

Use these tools in a way that works for you; as you'll see from the summary on pages 140 and 141, they can be used in a variety of ways and places. Some are likely to become everyday favourites; some might be used now and again; and others might not be used at all! The descriptions should enable you to try out most of the techniques on your own, though for some of the statistical tools, the text simply aims to introduce the broad concepts only, so you may need some support, at least to begin with.

The Improvement Journey follows a tried and tested eight-step improvement process, mapped against the Define, Measure, Analyse, Improve, Control (DMAIC), methodology. At the beginning of each step, you'll find a description, 'What's this step all about?' and a summary of 'the key outputs from this step'.

'Tollgate Reviews' at the end of each step enable you to take stock of progress and stay on track. To help you, there is a set of 'key questions before moving on' to the next step. The reviews are an essential element in ensuring success and identifying lessons. The diagram on the inside front cover highlights the importance of three additional Benefit Reviews at the end of Steps 3, 6 and 8. These reviews help ensure projects are scoped appropriately, and goals are achieved.

Some key principles

For the approach to be successful, it's vital to recognise the need for different thinking. This quote from Albert Einstein sums things up very well, "The significant problems we face cannot be solved by the same level of thinking which caused them." We want to change outcomes, but we need to realise that they are themselves the outcomes from our systems. Not the computer systems, but the way we work together and interact. And these systems are the product of how we think and behave. So, if we want to change the outcomes, we have to change our systems, and to do that, we have to change our thinking.

We need to adopt thinking that focuses on improving value for the customer, by improving and smoothing the process flow, and eliminating waste. Since Henry Ford's first production line, Lean Thinking has evolved through a number of sources, and over many years, but much of the development has been led by Toyota through the development of the 'Toyota Production System'. They were able to build on Ford's production ideas, moving from 'high volume, low variety', to high variety of choice with low volumes.

The five key principles of Lean Thinking are set out below:

- Understand the customer and their perception of value
- Identify and understand the value stream for each process and the waste within it
- Enable the value to flow
- Let the customer pull the value through the processes, according to their needs
- Continuously pursue perfection (continuous improvement)

Six Sigma thinking complements these principles through a systematic and robust approach to improvement that is based on management by fact and is also focused on the customer and key stakeholders. If we are to deliver the best customer experience, we have to listen to and understand the 'Voice of the Customer'. We can then make sure that the objectives of our services and processes are appropriately focused.

Measurement and management by fact enables more effective decision-making, and by understanding variation we'll also know when to take action and when not to. Of course, to be truly effective, we need to involve the people in the process, equipping them to be able, and feel able to challenge and improve their processes and the way they work.

The five key principles of Six Sigma are:

- Understand the critical to quality requirements (CTQs) of our customers and stakeholders
- Understand our processes ensuring they reflect these CTQs
- Manage by fact
- Involve and equip the people in the process
- Undertake improvement activity in a systematic way

As you can see, there is both similarity and synergy between Lean and Six Sigma, and a set of Lean Six Sigma key principles emerges.

The Magnificent Seven?

The key principles of Lean Six Sigma are:

- Focus on the customer
- Identify and understand how the work gets done – the value stream
- Manage, improve, and smooth the process flow
- Remove Non-Value-Add steps and waste
- Manage by fact and reduce variation
- Involve and equip the people in the process
- Undertake improvement activity in a systematic way

We've already made reference to 'involving the people', so let's look at these other elements in a little more detail:

- The key focus is on the customer. You need to understand their perception of value, and their CTQs. The CTQs provide the basis for your measurement set which will help you understand how well you are performing against these critical requirements.

  Focusing on the customer, and the concept of Value-Add, is especially important as typically, only 10 – 15% of process steps add value, and often represent only 1% of the total process time.

- By identifying and understanding how the work gets done – the value stream, you can highlight the Non-Value steps and waste. In doing so, you can ensure the process is focused on meeting the CTQs and adding value. To do this properly, you have to go to the 'Gemba'. This Japanese word is usually associated with the workplace – where the work gets done, or where the action is. And that's where management begins. Process Stapling involves doing just that to see how the work really gets done, not how we think it gets done, or how we'd like to think it gets done!

  So go to the workplace to see the real process being carried out, and collect data on what's happening. You'll find this will make it easier for you to analyse the problem in your DMAIC improvement project, and will help you determine a more effective solution.

  Understanding, managing and improving the value stream is key as it sets out all of the actions, both value creating and Non-Value creating, that bring a product or service concept to launch. And bring a customer order through supply chain processing to delivery. These include actions to process information from the customer, and actions to transform the product on its way to the customer.

  Toyota's Taiichi Ohno describes the approach very effectively: "All we are doing is looking at a time line from the moment the customer gives us an order to the point when we collect the cash. And we are reducing that time line by removing the Non-Value-Added wastes."

- Managing, improving and smoothing the process flow provides another example of different thinking. If possible use single piece flow, moving away from batches, or at least reducing batch sizes. Either way, identify the Non-Value-Added steps in processes and try to remove them – certainly look to ensure they do not delay Value-Adding steps. The concept of pull, not push, links to our understanding the process and improving flow. And it can be an essential element in avoiding bottlenecks. Overproduction or pushing things through too early is a waste.
- Removing Non-Value-Add steps and waste is another vital element in improving performance. One way to improve flow and performance, generally, is to identify, remove, and prevent waste or, as the Japanese call it, Muda. They describe two broad types and seven categories of waste.
- Managing by fact, using accurate data, will help you avoid jumping to conclusions and solutions. You need the facts! And that means measuring the right things in the right way. Data collection is a process and needs to be managed accordingly. Using Control Charts will enable you to interpret the data correctly and understand the process variation. You will then know when to take action and when not to.
- The action you take in improving your processes needs to be undertaken in a systematic way. The focus in this book, of course, is through DMAIC.

A separate book, the Six Sigma Design Journey covers the design of new products, services, and processes, where the five phases are **D**efine, **M**easure, **A**nalyse, **D**esign and **V**erify (DMADV).

DMAIC or DMADV?

DMAIC/DMADV transition points:

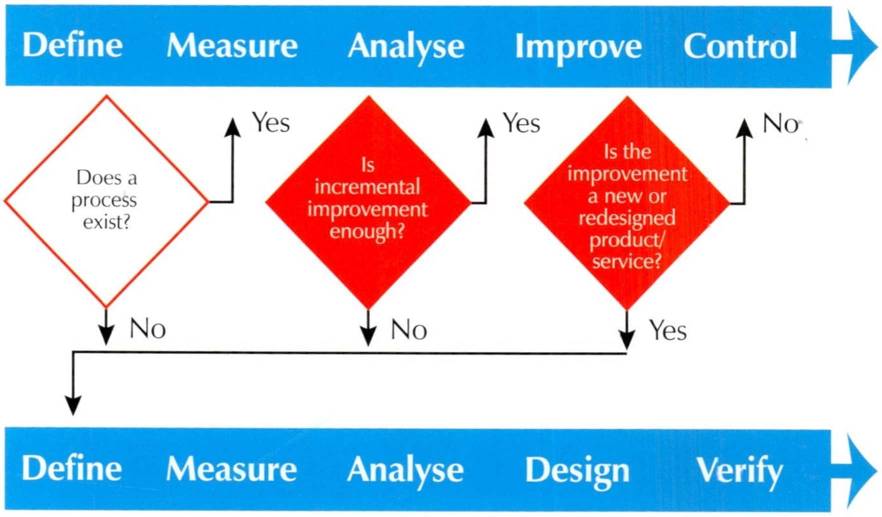

It is possible to start a project using the DMAIC methodology only to find yourself at some point changing to DMADV, as this high level picture shows.

So, Lean Six Sigma provides a rigorous and structured approach to help manage and improve performance. It helps you use the right tools, in the right place, and in the right way, not just in improvement and design projects, but also in your day-to-day activities. It really is about getting the key principles and concepts of Lean Six Sigma into the DNA and lifeblood of the organisation, so that it becomes a natural part of how you do things.

Pages 6 and 7 contain a Road Map outlining the step by step improvement method, and the key tools and techniques. To successfully manage your improvement projects, you will need to use at least some of these. But it doesn't matter how many you know and use, if you don't recognise the importance of the 'soft stuff'.

Managing change – the importance of the soft stuff

So what do we mean by the 'soft stuff'? In simple terms, it's about how well we work with the people involved in the process, and the stakeholders who are touched by the project. And it's about their acceptance of what you are trying to do. You may well have developed an ideal solution, but its effectiveness will be dependent on how well you have gained acceptance from your organisation.

George Eckes is Chief Executive Officer of a Colorado-based consulting group and a former psychologist. He came up with a formula to express this relationship: E = Q x A.

E = Effectiveness	This represents the effectiveness of the implementation which depends on the quality of the solution and the level of acceptance
Q = The quality of the solution	An ideal solution may have been identified, but its effectiveness will depend on how well it is accepted
A = The level of acceptance of the solution	The level of acceptance is key, as it has a multiple effect on the overall success of the implementation

It's outside the scope of this book to look at all of the aspects involved in Managing Change, but we have included a number of relevant tools and techniques to help you. These include, for example, the Improvement Charter, Stakeholder Analysis, the 3Ds Matrix, and De Bono's 'Thinking Hats'.

Although you will be monitoring the progress of the specific tasks of your project, it's sensible to also keep an eye how well you are doing with these softer elements.

Clearly, communication will be vital throughout the project, and it will be sensible to develop a Communication Plan that helps ensure you get the right messages to the right people at the right time, and in an appropriate medium.

DEFINE

Select the problem

DMAIC projects start with a problem that needs to be solved. You must ensure that everyone involved has a clear understanding of their role, why the project is being undertaken, and what it's trying to achieve.

Key outputs for step one

- Improvement Charter
- The CTQs
- SIPOC Diagram
- Stakeholder Analysis
- Elevator Speech
- Risk Assessment
- Storyboard
- Communications Plan

MEASURE

Understand the current situation

It's likely that the work you have done in Step 1 is based on what you think the problem is. Now you need to clarify things by understanding how the work gets done and how well it gets done.

Key outputs for step two

- Confirm the CTQs
- Confirm the SIPOC
- Deployment Flow-chart or
- Value Stream Map
- Output Measures (Ys)
- Input & Process Measures (Xs)
- Data Collection Plan
- SPC Control Charts
- Baseline Performance
- Updated Charter
- Updated Storyboard
- Updated Comms Plan

ANALYSE

Identify & check the possible causes

Now you know what's happening, it's time to generate ideas about why. But don't jump to conclusions. It's important to check the possible causes using data to verify the ideas generated, and manage by fact. In verifying the vital few, you may find 'the usual suspects' are not guilty at all! Identifying and removing the root causes of a problem will prevent it happening again.

Key outputs for step three

- Value-Add Analysis
- Identification of Waste
- Fishbone Diagram
- Confirmed X measures
- Data Displays
- The Root Cause
- Updated Charter
- Updated Storyboard
- Updated Comms Plan
- Stakeholder Analysis

IMPROVE

Select the solution

It's time to choose the most appropriate solution. In doing so, you will need to take account of the results from any testing or piloting, and the criteria you've identified as important. These are likely to include factors such as customer priorities, cost, speed and ease of implementation.

It may seem obvious, but make sure your solution addresses the problem and that customers will see a difference if it's adopted.

Key outputs for step five

- The Solution
- Draft Cost Analysis
- Updated Storyboard
- Updated Comms Plan
- Stakeholder Analysis

IMPROVE

Plan and test the solution

This step seeks to ensure the smooth implementation of your chosen solution. The main focus, though, is on prevention – causing something not to happen. Carrying out a more detailed pilot is likely to be helpful.

Key outputs for step six

- A Pilot
- Implementation Plan
- Updated Charter
- Updated Storyboard
- Updated Comms Plan
- Stakeholder Analysis

STEP 7

CONTROL

Implement, standardise and control

Depending on the scope of the project, implementation could be relatively simple or difficult. Either way, this step looks to help you ensure that you hold the gain.

All the key elements of Process Management should be coming together.

Key outputs for step seven

- The Solution in place
- Updated Documentation
- Training Plan
- Data Collection Plan
- SPC Control Chart
- Effective Handover
- Updated Storyboard
- Updated Comms Plan

STEP 4

IMPROVE

Generate possible solutions

Having identified the root cause of the problem you can generate ideas to tackle it, though the solution may be evident from the work done in the previous two steps.

Do make sure that your proposed solutions address the problem and its cause.

Key outputs for step four

- Potential Solutions
- New Deployment Flow-chart or;
- New Value Stream Map
- Updated Storyboard
- Updated Comms Plan

STEP 8

CONTROL

Assess achievements and lessons

This is where you take stock of what's been achieved and how. Depending on the nature of the project, you may need to prepare for a formal update to management.

Make sure you remember to recognise the efforts of the people who have been involved in the project.

And don't forget to, apply the learning from this project to the next one you tackle.

Key outputs for step eight

- Completed Storyboard
- Key Lessons
- Confirmation of Benefits
- Recommendations
- Next Steps
- Recognition

Before moving from one step to another, it will be important to step back, assess progress, and ask some key questions.

These will include:

- How are things going?
- Are we on course?
- What have we learnt?
- What's gone well, and why?
- What conclusions can be drawn?

The Tollgates also provide an opportunity to update the Improvement Charter and to take stock of the benefits and financials. Wherever you do that, ensure you document the assumptions made.

Because of their importance the three 'Benefit Reviews' are highlighted on the inside front cover of this book.

Before the project began, you will probably have best guessed a business case that justifies starting the work. By the end of Step 3, you should be able to 'Quantify the Opportunity'. You will know what's happening and why, and should be able to determine how much the Non-Value-Added work is costing, and how it is stopping you meeting the CTQs. This will enable you to scope the project appropriately.

In Step 5, you'll select the most appropriate solution. Once you've carried out a Pilot in Step 6, you should be able to confirm the benefits. The Final Review enables you to confirm the actual costs and benefits and whether there have been any unexpected debits or credits. And you should know the answers to these questions:

- Do your customers feel there has been an improvement? How do you know?
- Are there lessons, ideas or 'best practices' that can be applied elsewhere in the business?

Taking time for these reviews and tollgates is an important element in developing a culture that manages by fact. So, take the opportunity – it will help ensure your projects are successful and the benefits are delivered. Maintaining an up to date Storyboard will help you prepare for the reviews and share lessons.

Step 1 – Select the problem

What's this step all about?

When you start any new improvement project, an essential ingredient for success will be for you to ensure that you and your team have a clear understanding of why the project is being undertaken, and what it's trying to achieve. With a DMAIC project, you start with a problem that needs to be solved.

Before you can solve it, however, you need to clearly define it, and that's not always as straightforward as it might sound. One of the key outputs from the Define phase, and one that will help you define the problem is a completed Improvement Charter. We'll look at this shortly, but depending on the nature of the project, you may need to use some other tools first.

Ideally, your project will be bite-sized, but if it's a large and potentially complex project, the Affinity Diagram can help you prepare for success. Certainly it will help you develop the Improvement Charter. The Affinity and Interrelationship Diagrams provide definition. In many ways, the Affinity Diagram can be seen as step zero in a large project, helping a team develop their thoughts of the issues involved. And by the time they have created the Interrelationship Diagram, the team will almost certainly have a detailed understanding of what needs to be done, the drivers of success, and the many and varied interrelationships involved. We've referenced the Interrelationship Diagram a little later in the book, showing you how it also links to the Fishbone Diagram in the Analyse phase.

Throughout your project it will make sense to develop a Storyboard summary of the key decisions and outputs – it will help you review progress and share your lessons. And, of course it will also help with at least some of the communication needed. Developing and reviewing a Communications Plan will be an essential activity for you – remember the E = Q x A formula!

So, whether you need to use the Affinity Diagram or not, let's look at the various outputs needed:

The key outputs from this step

- A first draft Improvement Charter that includes:
    - A Business Case
    - A Problem Statement
    - A Goal Statement
    - The Project Scope
    - High Level Milestones
    - Agreed Roles And Responsibilities
- The CTQs, or at least a plan to agree them. This may need to be carried over into the Measure phase
- A SIPOC Diagram, providing a high level map of the process
- A Stakeholder Analysis – remember the importance of the soft stuff!
- An Elevator Speech is likely to prove helpful, but may not always be necessary
- An assessment of the risks to the project
- A Storyboard
- A Communications Plan

Key questions before moving on

- What's the purpose of this project? What are we trying to do?
- How will customers be affected by the successful completion of this project?
- Do we have the CTQs in place? If not, how do we plan to agree them?
- How will we know if things improve?
- Are we happy that everyone understands their roles and responsibilities?
- What data or information is missing?
- Have we thought through the risks?
- Who should we be communicating with? What should we be telling them, and when, and how should we be doing it?

Key tools for this step

Affinity Diagram

The purpose of the Affinity Diagram is to generate, pull together and organise, a potentially extensive and unorganised amount of information. This could be a mixture of facts, opinions, ideas and intuitions, but the technique leads to consensus and ownership of the way forward on usually quite large issues and projects.

Let's open things up...

Essentially, it is a silent brainstorm on a grand scale. But there's a difference, as the steps below show. In using the technique with the Fishbone Diagram, you try to keep the issue statement (in the head of the fish), quite narrow. You don't want a whalebone diagram! As 'step zero' in your project, you want to open things up, to generate as many ideas and issues as possible. So:

1. Take time to agree an issue statement or question to brainstorm around. Clearly define what the statement or question means and, perhaps, what it doesn't mean. Everyone must agree on the statement or question before you can proceed. These usually begin with words like:
   - "Factors that influence"
   - "Elements of"
   - "What are the issues involved in?"
   - "What are the barriers or problems involved in?"
   - "What makes x effective?"

2. Silently brainstorm the ideas, capturing each idea on a Post-it. There should only be one idea per Post-it, written clearly to ensure everyone can read it. One word entries aren't very helpful, usually, but nor are those with too many words. Using a noun and verb will help.

There are no crowns to mend, but plenty of brown paper helps...

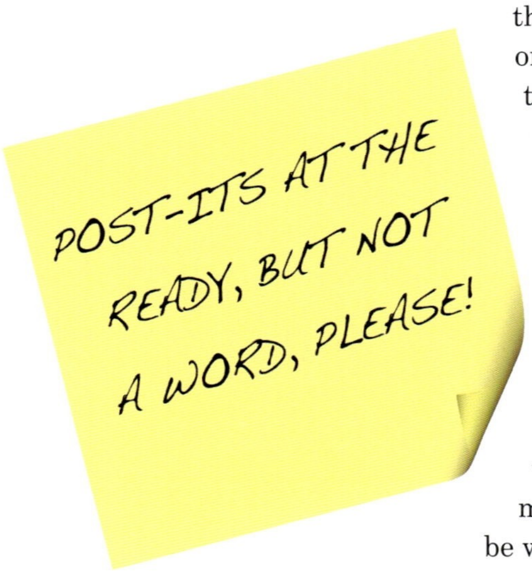

3. When everyone has finished writing, the process of clustering can begin. But only when everyone has finished. Once they have, everyone, all at the same time, and still in silence, puts their various Post-its on the wall and in any order they wish! It helps to have some large sheets of brown paper on the wall.

4. It's time to step back, possibly in amazement, and read the different entries, still in silence! Reading the various Post-its might prompt some more ideas and additional Post-its can be written at any stage.

5. This next step can be quite entertaining. Everyone, all at the same time and still in silence, can start to move the Post-its around, putting them into what they perceive to be groups or clusters of similar ideas or themes. Some of these might be quite lateral, rather than the more traditional headings associated with the Fishbone, for example.

6. There might be some stragglers at this stage; Post-its with no apparent home. Don't worry about them just yet, but don't forget about them either.

Remember, at any stage, additional Post-its can be written; and there might well be a case for one idea to appear more than once and in different clusters.

It might also be appropriate to break the silence; the facilitator will determine the right time to do this. Almost certainly there will be a need to clarify what's meant by an idea or a Post-it, or the thoughts behind a particular grouping that's emerging. The facilitator will also determine when it's appropriate to move to the next step in the process.

7. This looks to agree a definition or description for each of the clusters and produce 'a header'. This may sound easy, but unlike the headers in the Fishbone Diagram, one-word titles will almost certainly be inadequate. The headers will need to 'stand on their own' when they are used in the Interrelationship Diagram. So, take your time and ensure they accurately describe the content of the cluster.

8. Back to the stragglers without a home. There are three possible actions:

    - You might find a home now the headers have been agreed for the others
    - A single Post-it might well form its own cluster and some further brainstorming could then generate some ideas to go with it, or, if everyone agrees...
    - A Post-it could be binned!

That sense of ownership and understanding increases significantly with the use of the Interrelationship Diagram. You will also find that a Tree Diagram is an effective way of developing your post-its into assignable actions.

In conjunction with the Tree Diagram, the Affinity Diagram can also prove a very effective way to pull together 'Voice of the Customer' comments and inputs, and identify high-level themes for action. You'll find an example of this on pages 114-115.

Key tools for this step

Improvement Charter

Knowing where you're going

When you first start an improvement journey, it's very easy to rush off in the wrong direction and waste time. The Improvement Charter will help you avoid that by providing a clear description of your project and what you hope to achieve.

It will also help you identify some of the additional information and data you will need to complete the journey. As you find out some of these, you will need to update and amend your Charter – often the first draft will be at quite a high level. As you progress through the steps, you will find the need to review and update your Charter as you discover even more about your problem and its likely solution.

An Improvement Charter should not be complicated or bureaucratic. Try to keep it simple, ideally using no more than a side or two of A4. A template is included on page 17, and, as you will see, there are a number of elements that need to be built into the document. These include:

- **A high level business case** – providing an explanation of why it's important to do this project
- **A problem statement** – remember that a DMAIC project starts with a problem
- **A goal statement** – describing the objective of the project
- **The project scope** – defining the parameters and identifying any constraints. The template refers to 'In Frame and Out of Frame', linking to the technique described on page 18
- **The CTQs** and a definition of a defect
- **Roles** – identifying the people involved in and around the project, the expectations of them, and their responsibilities
- **Milestones** – a high level summary of the key steps and dates to achieve the goal

Let's look at some of these elements in a little more detail:

So what's the point?

The Business Case describes the broad area(s) of concern for an improvement team project and the rationale for doing it. So:

- why is this project worth doing?
- why is it important to do it now?
- what are the consequences of not doing it?
- how does it fit with the business strategy, initiatives and targets?

In agreeing this, your team will understand the business imperative for the project and you will also know why it's been selected ahead of other potential activities. Naturally, the project Champion has a key role in this aspect.

The Problem Statement describes what's wrong: So, in terms of problems:

What's wrong?

- what is wrong or not meeting our customer's requirements?
- when and where do the problems occur?
- how big is the problem?
- what's the impact of the problem?

Early on in the project, you may not have enough information or data to provide all the detail you'd like. Remember that your whole approach to improvement should be based on fact, so if you don't yet have the information, don't guess it! Leave gaps or keep things at a high level; you can update the Improvement Charter later on.

You will soon discover that working on the Charter quickly helps you identify the information and measurements needed on the project.

The Goal Statement should focus on the results or impact you hope to achieve. It should not make assumptions about the causes of the problem; nor should it prescribe the solution!

And what's better?

Ideally, it should start with a verb, for example:

- increase
- reduce
- eliminate
- control

And there should be a measurable target and completion date.

In checking the effectiveness of your Charter's Problem and Goal Statements, make sure they are **SMART**:

Get Smart!

- **S**pecific
- **M**easurable
- **A**ttainable
- **R**elevant
- **T**ime bound

The Project Scope defines the boundaries and resources of the team's improvement effort. If the scope is too broad, a team can waste effort by proposing solutions that are outside its influence or resource capability.

Setting the boundaries

But if the scope is too narrow, it can lead to limited and often disappointing solutions. It's a question of balance.

The following questions should help clarify things:

- what processes will the team focus on?
- what are the boundaries of the process you aim to improve?
- what's the start point and end point?
- what resources are available to the team?
- what, if anything, is out of bounds for the team?
- what, if any, constraints must the team work under?
- what is the time commitment that's expected of the team members?
- and what happens to their 'regular duties' while they are working on the project?

When will you get there?

Milestones are needed for the key steps and activities on your journey. They should provide a sense of urgency and a feeling of accomplishment. But like the Goal Statement, they should also be SMART.

Again, it's worth remembering that these will probably be high level best guesses at the start of the project. As you get a clearer picture of what will be needed for your journey they should become more accurate.

Who's doing what?

'Roles' is a key element in the Improvement Charter.

It doesn't matter how many improvement tools and techniques you know inside out, if the team doesn't work well together, the project will not succeed.

Well defined roles help ensure smooth working relationships within the team, and with key influencers in the organisation. The following questions might help you clarify things up front:

- how do you want the Champion to work with the team?
- is the team's role to implement or recommend?
- when must the team seek approval from the Champion?
- what authority does the team have to act independently?
- what and how do you want to inform the Champion about the team's progress?
- what is the role of the improvement team leader?
- what is the role of the coach or mentor?
- in terms of both function and hierarchy, are the right people on the team?

You might want to use GRIP or RACI to help you clarify and agree things.

Improvement Charter Template

Project title:	Date commenced:

Why *High level business case describing why this project is important and how it links to our business plans*

What *The problem and goal statements, the scope, and the CTQ and defect definitions for the relevant customers and processes*

Problem statement	Goal statement
In frame	Out of frame
CTQs	Defect definition

Who *The process owner, Champion, team leader, and team members. Who are they and what are their roles, responsibilities, and time commitments? What involvement is expected of the Champion? How often should they meet?*

Name	Roles & responsibilities	Time commitment

When *High level timeframes for the phases. This could be mapped to the eight steps.*

	Date	Date	Date	Date	Date	Date
Define						
Measure						
Analyse						
Improve						
Control						

Only fifteen words?

Fifteen Word Flipchart

The 'Fifteen Word Flipchart' can help in developing the problem and goal statements. This involves people using a Post-it to draft their own statements of the problem, for example, in a maximum of 15 words. When these are put up on the flipchart, the team can highlight key phrases or words that need to be encompassed within the eventual Improvement Charter statements.
Naturally, the final statement can be as many words as you need.

This technique can also be helpful in drafting the Elevator Speech, and in determining the project scope...

Lets avoid the creep!

In Frame/Out of Frame

As with so many things, it helps if you start off on the right foot. One of the most important things in managing a project is to have a clear understanding of the scope. Even when you do, 'scope creep' is still pretty hard to avoid; but without it, you have little chance of doing so.

The In Frame/Out of Frame tool provides a simple visual technique to help teams and Stakeholders get a clear picture of what's included and what isn't. This might cover a range of things, including, for example:

- The customer and market segments
- The products and services
- The processes involved
- The people affected
- The computer systems involved
- The type and extent of the improvement results that are expected

The In Frame/Out of Frame tool may provide a helpful framework at an early team meeting to clarify what's already been drafted in the Improvement Charter.

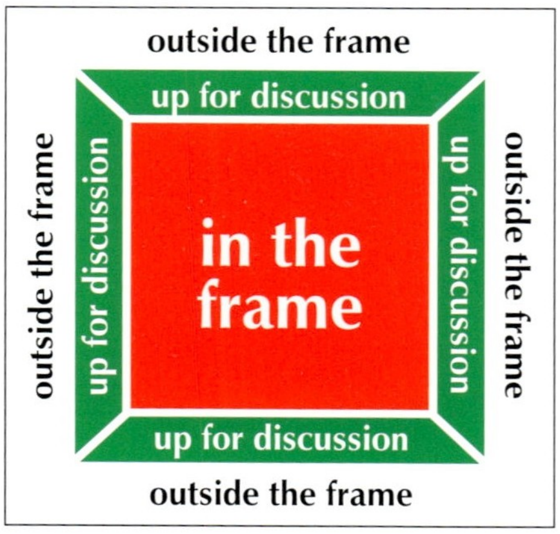

The process is straightforward:

- A picture frame is drawn onto a flipchart
- The various issues are brainstormed and written onto Post-its
- These are placed in what appears to be the most appropriate position
- The issues are then reviewed and discussed

So, do you get the picture?

So, things are either in the frame (within scope), or they're not (outside of scope). Involving the Champion will be especially helpful in clarifying the items 'up for discussion'.

Thinking Hats

Let's take our hat off to De Bono…

Edward De Bono's Six Thinking Hats [Six Thinking Hats, Penguin, 1985], reflect the six different ways of thinking.

Before covering these different modes of thinking let's put them into a context you are probably familiar with. Meetings!

Meetings where a meeting of minds simply isn't on the agenda.

Meetings often fail because the people involved are thinking in different modes at different times during the proceedings. It's pretty well impossible to reach sensible decisions when, and at the same time…

- One person is trying to explain the situation and describe what's happened
- A second is buzzing with bright ideas, some of which may be highly appropriate
- A third is killing the ideas at birth, including the ones that might well have worked
- Another is thinking: "no way is that happening in my area!"

And so on. The Chair has no idea what's going on, other than it's not a very constructive meeting, and it closes with most, if not all of the participants feeling pretty frustrated. Been there, done that?

The Thinking Hats provide a framework to help overcome these problems and improve meetings, generally.

So you think you know about thinking...?

The six different ways of thinking are:

Factual –

- "These are the numbers sold."
- "The supplier has done this."
- "The customers are complaining about it."
- "The customers aren't going to like this" isn't a fact, unless they've told you beforehand and you can evidence it, perhaps with research data.

Emotional –

- "No way is that happening in my area!"
- "We should be selling tons of the stuff."

Optimistic –

- This describes the benefits of a proposal, the "what's in it for us" type statements.
- "We'll be able to cut costs and increase customer satisfaction."
- "Our market share could increase to x%."

Creativity –

- This covers ideas and 'blue skying'.
- "What if we designed an oojamaflip?"

Critical –

- "That will work only if..."
- "That won't work because..."
- "This has to be done, too..."

Thinking about thinking –

- This is about planning the meeting, for example, and the Chair will be determining which hat to wear and when.
- "We'll start the meeting by reviewing the facts, or by identifying the facts we need, then we'll discuss the benefits of re-launching the product."

'Hats' are a good description for these thinking modes and De Bono created the idea of using different coloured hats to represent them.

- White – facts we know or need to know
- Red – emotion
- Yellow – optimism
- Green – creativity
- Black – constructive criticism based on analysis
- Blue – planning

People soon become reasonably happy with the idea of 'wearing' these different hats and the Chair or facilitator can conduct the discussion more effectively by determining the thinking modes to be used at different points in the meeting.

Whether you use the hats analogy or the colours is up to you. If you do, you don't need to use every colour every time; you don't need to use the hats all the time. But they can become part of the common language and be used even when using another technique. In starting a project, a good first session could be:

- Factual – what's the situation?
- Emotional – developing the Problem or Goal Statement.
- Optimistic – the benefits of the project.

Taking this approach could be helpful in developing the first draft of your Improvement Charter.

What do you think your favourite colour is?

It's the concept that's important

Customers need to get their requirements across

CTQs

We have made several references to the Voice of the Customer (VOC) and to CTQs. It might be that you already have these in place, but if not, you will need to do so, either as part of Step 1, or more likely, in Step 2 as you seek to understand the current situation.

There are a large number of sources for VOC, including market research, focus groups, surveys and complaints. The trick is to translate what the customer has said into a measurable requirement – the CTQ. To do this properly will probably involve a number of conversations, both with the customer and the process owner, and with the people in the process, and your interpretations need to be reflected back to ensure they are correct.

Essentially, you need to gather input from the customers to understand their needs. You have to identify their key issues, and translate them into terms that are meaningful and measurable. But, remember this is about determining requirements, not solutions.

The Matrix below provides a framework for the process. In the first example, there seem to be two key issues, getting through to the right person, and speed. You would need to go back to the customer and agree what 'quickly' means. A second measurable requirement might then be: 'the call is answered within 10 seconds', for example.

Voice of the Customer	Key issue(s)	CTQ
You either put me on hold, or put me through to the wrong department or person	The customer wants to be put through quickly to the right person	■ Customer gets through to the correct person the first time
You send me an invoice at different times of the month	Consistent monthly billing	■ Customer bill received same day of the month
It takes too long to process my mortgage application and get me the money when it's needed	Speed up loan so I get the money on time	■ Customer receives cheque on customer request date

The Affinity Diagram and the Tree Diagram provide useful formats for sorting VOC information into themes, and then into more detailed elements.

Getting the CTQs right is essential, since not only do they help ensure you are correctly focusing on the customer requirements, they also provide the foundation for your measurement data.

SIPOC *Understanding Processes – developing a high level SIPOC*

A process is a series of steps and actions that produce a product or a service. All work is a process, and a process is a blend of people, equipment, method, materials, and environment. This description of processes applies to everything we do, from getting up in the morning, to making a cup of tea, to paying a customer's pension, for example.

All work is a process

All of these activities can be broken down as a series of steps.

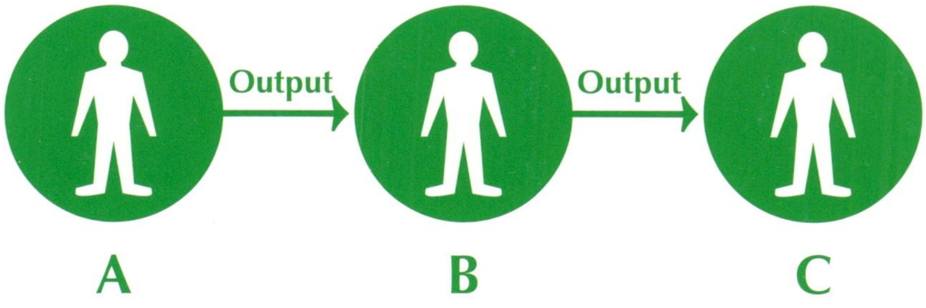

When we do that we start to recognise that processes involve other people, and at work, these other people can be described as internal customers and suppliers.

Department A produces output for Department B, who produce output for Department C, who provide the answer to an external customer enquiry, for example. What's important here is to recognise that all of these departments are involved in the process and need to understand the objectives of the 'big process'. All too often each of the departments will be working in a vacuum.

Processes should be 'adding value' for the customer and should be seeking to meet their requirements. If that is to happen it is important to recognise that the process itself has requirements that need to be met.

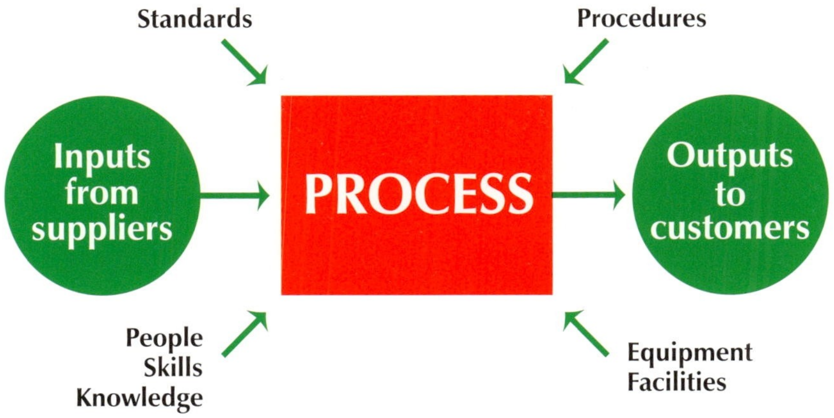

Processes have requirements too

- The first requirement of a process is to ensure that the customer's requirements are understood and agreed. More often than not, a lack of quality or re-work are the direct result of not defining these properly. Even on apparently simple things, a little extra time spent in translating the 'Voice of the Customer' and clarifying requirements will help save time and potential upset later on
- Once the customer's requirements have been agreed, the next step is to determine your own requirements from suppliers. The same 'rules' apply. Spend the time to ensure these are properly understood and agreed
- You will need to ensure the right number of people are working in the process, and that they have the necessary knowledge and skills. If they don't, appropriate training needs to be delivered
- The procedures must be developed, agreed, appropriately documented and kept up to date. Importantly, they should be simple to follow and understand. Clear English and 'pictures' will help ensure they're used to good effect
- Standards will apply including, for example, regulatory requirements or service level agreements, and will need to be clearly communicated, too. Like procedures these should be documented in a way that's easy to understand. Similarly, if there's a budget involved or authority limits on certain actions, then management must ensure the people in the process know the details
- Equipment and facilities will be needed to operate the process. These must be appropriate from day one, located in the right place and correctly maintained, thereafter. In other words, ensure the right equipment is in the right place and is regularly serviced and updated. And ensure the environment is appropriate for the activity

The 'process model' evolves from the SIPOC Diagram – one of the key Step 1 outputs.

SIPOC helps us begin with the end in mind…

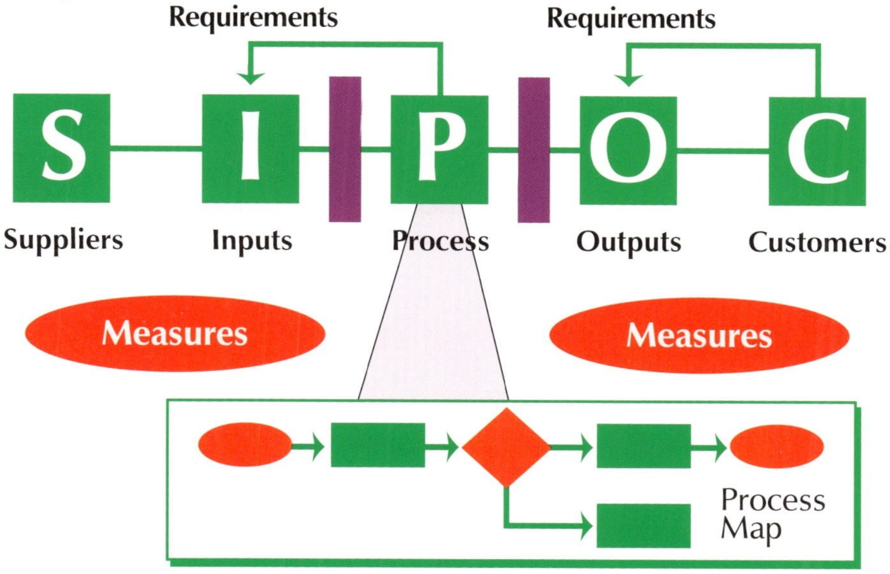

The SIPOC model identifies the customers and the outputs they need, presents a high level Process Map, usually comprising four to eight steps, and confirms your input requirements from suppliers. Remember, that the customer can also be a supplier, particularly of information needed by you.

The model also provides a framework to determine the measurement data needed in Step 2.

The diagram below provides the basis of a SIPOC template.

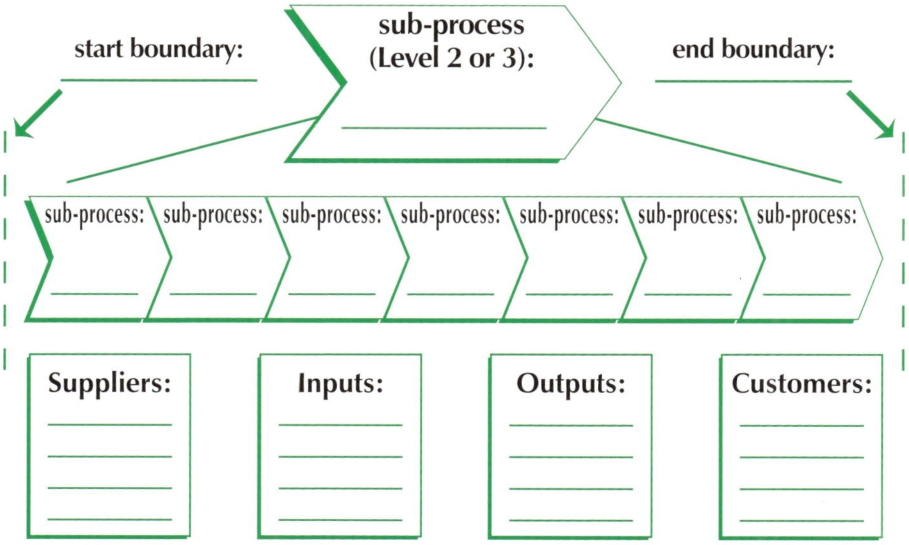

Building your SIPOC

Incidentally, it's probably fair to say that the model should be referred to as COPIS, since you must begin its development with the customer and their requirements; and that means you must be listening to the customer.

and with the end in mind…

So who's in favour?

Stakeholder Analysis

No matter what the issue is, some people will be very much for it; some completely against; and some in-between. There will probably be others who don't seem to be particularly interested one way or the other. And that's pretty much life!

So, you shouldn't be surprised when you find this picture applying to your project, or to the solution that you and your team have eventually developed. And if you can't see that picture, then you better find out what the situation looks like, both on the surface and beneath it.

This tool helps teams develop a detailed sense of who the key stakeholders are, how they currently feel about the change initiative, and the level of support they need to exhibit for the change initiative to have a good chance for success. It also helps the team begin to discover ways to influence relationships and develop strategies that will be effective for each key stakeholder.

The first thing to do is to identify the stakeholders – using a Force Field Diagram may help. A key stakeholder is anyone who controls critical resources, who can block the change initiative by direct or indirect means, who must approve certain aspects of the change strategy, who shapes the thinking of other critical parties, or who owns a key work process impacted by the change initiative. So:

- Who are they?
- Where do they currently stand on the issues associated with this change initiative?
- Are they supportive?
- How supportive?
- Are they against?
- And how much against?
- Or are they broadly neutral?

Given their status or influence on your project, where do you need them to be? It may be both desirable and possible to move some stakeholders to a higher level of support. How will you do that? What are their 'hot and cold buttons'? How can you present the project in a more appealing and effective way for them?

You won't need everyone to be in favour...

Sometimes it may be entirely appropriate for them to be in a neutral position. And every now and then, it might be appropriate to scale down someone's support!

The Matrix provides a framework to capture and present your perceptions. You would begin by mapping your perceptions of their current position.

Stakeholder Matrix

Names	Strongly against	Moderately against	Neutral	Moderately supportive	Strongly supportive	Hot/cold spots

List each stakeholder along the left side of the chart and proceed to discuss where you feel each one is currently. In discussing each individual, examine both objective evidence of where the individual is, as well as subjective opinion.

How do you rate the stakeholders?

It may be useful to first have each team member rate each stakeholder without discussion, and then tally individual ratings and discuss obvious differences. While it probably isn't critical to strive for complete consensus, it is usually worth taking the time to generally agree on whether each stakeholder is against, neutral, or supportive.

Once this is agreed, the discussion turns to where each stakeholder needs to be for the change initiative to be successful. Remember, some stakeholders may need only to be shifted to neutral to stop them being an active blocker. It will not be necessary for everyone to be strongly supportive.

How do you get them where you want them?

The next step is to develop an effective strategy for influencing them in order to increase, or at least, maintain their level of support. This is where the hot and cold buttons come into play.

Sometimes it will be a simple matter of presenting information in the right way for a particular person. Some will prefer lots of detail; others will want only a high level summary. Some will want facts and figures; others will prefer pictures.

Whatever the approach, careful thought needs to be given to who will have most impact on a particular stakeholder, what is the nature of the message that needs to be delivered, and how and when the influence process should begin.

Who can help?

In determining ways to move the stakeholders, remember there may be help available from those who are supporters of the initiative. A strongly supportive key stakeholder might also be a thought leader for others on your list. How can you enlist their support in shaping the thinking of other less supportive stakeholders?

Stakeholder Analysis can be used throughout the project, including, for example, agreeing ways to bring on board a new stakeholder who has just emerged.

The good, the bad, and the ugly...

Finally, remember that mapping where you feel stakeholders are, is not about good and bad, or right and wrong. Assessing things in that way would be potentially destructive.

Try to focus on how key individuals view the merits of the change initiative, and why. Someone may be strongly against a change initiative for what they feel are very good reasons (just as each of us is either for, against, or neutral on something).

Avoiding this tendency to see the rating as good or bad is critical to getting the most from this tool, enabling you to more effectively develop appropriate influencing strategies.

If there is the tendency within the team to label people, it might be better to avoid the rating element and simply discuss whether key stakeholders are for this initiative or against it.

Three Ds Matrix

Have you got 3D vision?

Of course, one of the things that will help bring people on board is to create a shared need. Developing a vision is certainly part of that process, but helping people see the evidence for themselves, can be particularly useful. The Three Ds Matrix provides a framework to help capture the evidence you currently have and identify where further evidence is needed. All of this can help you encourage the change and address the potential concerns of stakeholders.

Walking the talk

The Three Ds	Examples, evidence, and actions
Data	Is existing benchmarking data available? This could be within your organisation or through one of your networking associations
Demonstrate	Where can you find examples of successful DMAIC projects? Is there a best practice site we can look at?
Demand	This is about leaders, especially the Champions and process owners walking the talk, and demanding appropriate behaviours and standards

Force Field Analysis

Force Field Analysis helps identify those 'forces' for and against change; the supporting and driving forces in favour, and the resisting barriers against.

These are brainstormed and appear either side of a vertical line drawn down the centre of the chart as this example shows:

Force Field Analysis of morale in department, where current perception is 'low'; should be 'high'.

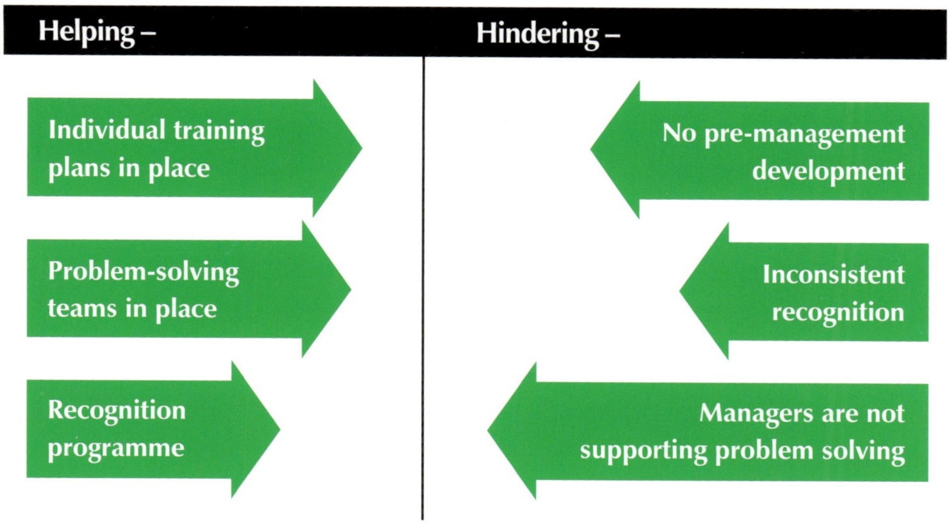

When the various issues have been brainstormed, discuss the relative strength of their 'force' and draw arrows to correspond. The longer the arrow, the stronger the force. You might want to incorporate a simple measurement scale.

You can then discuss and agree ways to (i) build on the positive forces and maximise their potential, and (ii) reduce or remove the negative barriers and constraining forces.

You should find the Force Field a helpful way of identifying the pros and cons of your improvement project, or the potential solution, for example.

Some of the drivers or barriers could be people, and you will need to develop strategies and tactics to capitalise or overcome them as the case may be. Creating a Force Field Diagram is often the first step in developing a Stakeholder Analysis.

One of Isaac Newton's Laws is at the root of this tool:

"For every force, there is an equal and opposite force."

A positive force often has an opposing negative force.

Are you with us or agin' us?

"The truth is out there somewhere..."

XY Grid

One way to help determine priorities for action is to present information in an 'XY Grid,' sometimes referred to as a Boston Box. The example provides a means of identifying performance against the customer's priorities for a service or product.

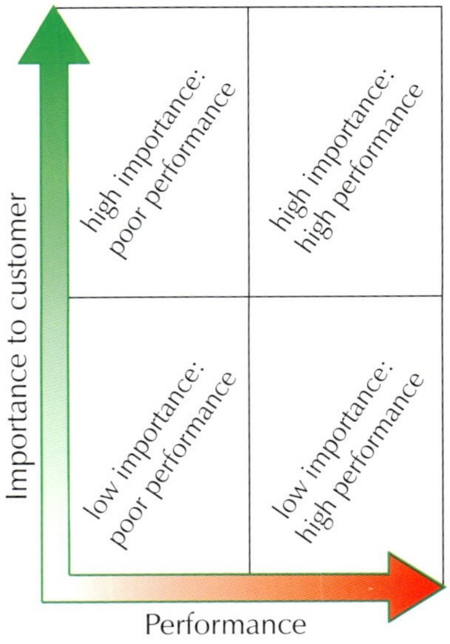

Naturally, you are looking for high performance against the customer's priority requirements. If you are not achieving that, but are performing well in an area of low priority, it might be sensible to review the allocation of resources.

Either way, by determining the importance of the customer's requirements and the capability of your processes, you can quickly determine your own priorities for improvement.

And of course, the XY Grid also works well with the Stakeholder Analysis by plotting the 'Level of support' against the 'Level of influence'.

The XY Grid is also appropriate to present a range of other items, including the results from a self assessment against the EFQM's Excellence Model.

The 'importance' aspect, here, would relate to your priorities.

Other options include 'ease of implementation' for improvement solutions against the 'importance to the business' of solving problems or the 'level of benefits' anticipated.

Backwards Visioning

Painting pictures…

Visions paint a picture that appeals to hearts and minds, and help answer the question, "why change?" In developing the desired state from the perspective of our customers, the business, and our employees, we are effectively developing a future vision that we are working towards.

A vision should provide a clear statement about the outcomes of the change effort, and in doing so, helps identify at least some of the elements that need to be changed. Visions secure commitment and support by helping people understand what it is that has to be done, and why.

Often, the vision will look at things in terms of the performance of our products and services, and the processes that support them. But we need to also consider some of the softer issues of behaviours.

Backwards Visioning provides a helpful framework to develop influencing strategies. And there are clear links to Stakeholder Analysis and the development of our Elevator Speech.

Use your imagination

It seeks to create a picture of the future that is expressed in behavioural terms. Improvement teams need to imagine their change has been successfully completed. If that were the case, what would they expect to see, both internally and externally, in terms of, for example:

- Behaviours?
- Measures?
- Rewards?
- Recognition?

What do we need more or less of?

In determining the team's perceptions of these issues, you can begin to understand the actions that need to be taken as part of your progress towards the desired state. These will include the activities and behaviours that we need to reduce and remove; and the ones we need to introduce and increase.

Have you got a minute?

Elevator Speech

Whether you are in the lift, at the coffee machine, or just about anywhere else, having a clear and simple project pitch up your sleeve is pretty handy. You never know who you might bump into. And if it's someone who is key to your project in some way, then the prepared and rehearsed pitch can help you secure their support and commitment. And it works just as effectively with securing support for the eventual solution that you and your team select.

The pitch should describe:

- The project (or solution)
- The need for change
- The vision of the new desired state that you are working towards
- What you would like from others

The term Elevator Speech is based around the idea that you might be in the lift and have a minute to make your pitch. The key is to keep it simple, and keep it short. But do make sure it's relevant, too.

Understanding and commitment going up

The lift's a great place for a last minute rehearsal!

You can put it to the test with your colleagues in the team. Indeed, developing the pitch with the team is a very good way of helping you all understand the project and increase your own commitment to it.

You might well get each member to write their own version and then compare notes, either choosing the best, or taking elements from each.

Fifteen words to the fore again

The Fifteen Word Flipchart can help with this.

Singing the same song

Finally, do make sure you all practice the delivery. This will help ensure that the message is delivered confidently and consistently by the whole team. After all, it's your sales opportunity and needs to be taken!

Getting a grip

GRIP

GRIP is a really simple tool that can be used by the project team at any stage in the project to review how the team is working together. It's a simple assessment process, best carried out separately by individuals on the team. You can then share your results together. Look for areas of commonality and difference in views. Look for areas of strength and weakness. Use your skills of facilitation to identify and agree improvement actions that will address any issues and improve team performance.

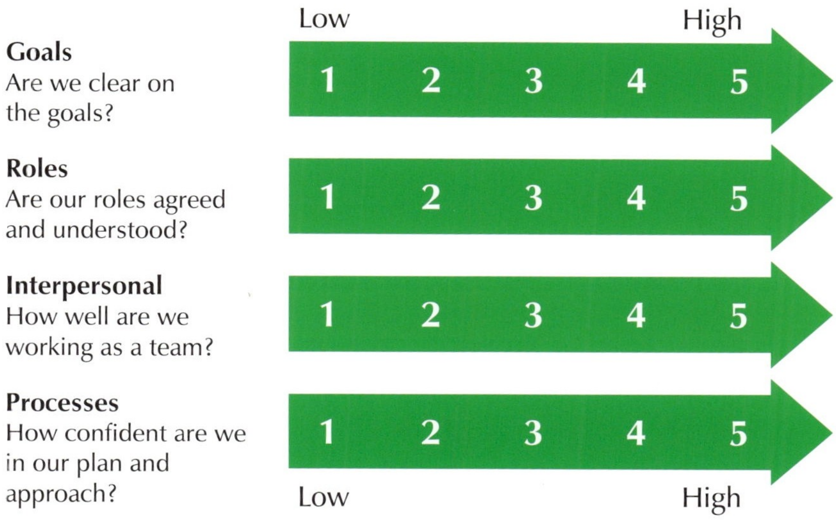

Thinking about your own project, you might want to carry out an assessment and identify whether any actions are needed. It could be that the high level questions shown in the diagram above will be sufficient, but a more comprehensive set of questions is set out on the next page.

		Low › › › › › › › › High				
		1	2	3	4	5
G	**Purpose & Outcomes** We understand and agree on our project mission and the desired outcome (vision) **Customer & Needs** We know who the project stakeholders are, what they require, and why this project is really needed **Goals & Deliverables** We have identified specific, measurable and prioritised project goals and deliverables linked to our business plans **Project Scope Definition** We understand/agree on what is in/out of our project scope and tasks. The project scope is ‘set’					
		Low › › › › › › › › High				
		1	2	3	4	5
R	**Roles & Responsibilities** We have defined and agreed on our roles, responsibilities, required skills and resources for the project team **Authority & Autonomy** Our team is clear on the degree of authority/empowerment we have to meet our project mission					
		Low › › › › › › › › High				
		1	2	3	4	5
I	**Team ‘Operating Agreement’** We have shared expectations, and agreed and followed guidelines for how our team works together **Interpersonal/Team** We have the necessary relationships, trust, openness, participation and behaviours for a healthy and productive team					
		Low › › › › › › › › High				
		1	2	3	4	5
P	**Critical Success Factors** We know and are focusing on the key factors needed to meet the project goals and mission **Plans & Activities** We have an effective plan to follow that includes the right tasks; these are clearly defined/assigned **Monitoring & Measures** We have an effective monitoring process and specific metrics linked to progress and goals **Schedule/Milestones** We have defined our project schedule and know what the key phases and milestones are					

PDPC (Process Decision Programme Chart)

The PDPC has a wide range of uses that all seek to encourage the adoption of preventive thinking, of causing something not to happen.

The PDPC is very easy to use and links with the Tree Diagram.

Essentially, it looks to identify what might go wrong, how could you prevent it, and what would you do if it still goes wrong?

It is commonly used to identify what might go wrong with a project, and, in particular, the implementation of a plan.

The framework is set out below:

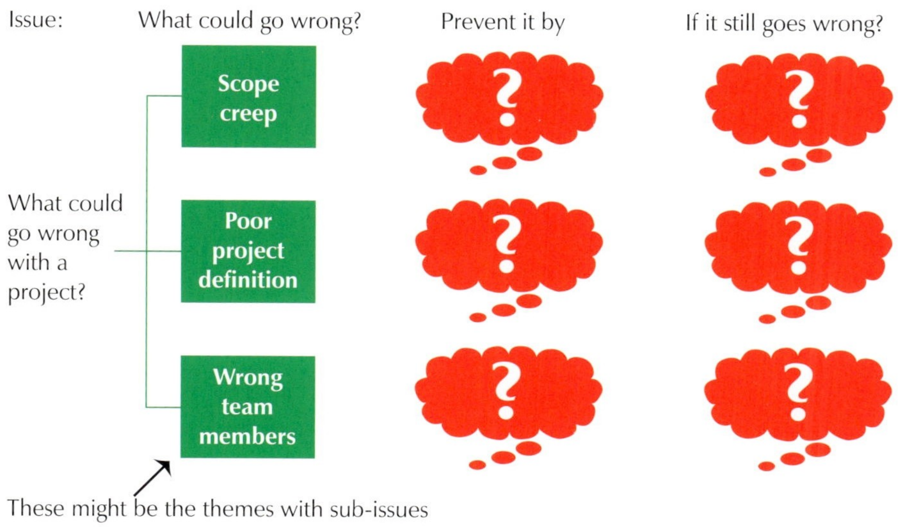

So, what might go wrong with your project, how could you prevent it, and what would you do if it still goes wrong?

You can generate your ideas through discussion or brainstorming. Negative Brainstorming is a particularly good way of doing this – how can you ensure 'this project' goes wrong?

Once you've identified what could go wrong, you can develop your ideas to prevent it happening, or to at least reduce the risk. But just in case it still happens, you will need to also determine what to do as a contingency.

There are lots of potential pitfalls and risks to any project, so carrying out a risk assessment is important. And not just at the beginning of the project, either; take time to review the risks throughout the project cycle.

Define – a quick summary

So, you've finished Define – at least for the moment. It's likely, you'll need to return to it as your understanding of the problem and the process increases. Either way, please remember that you might not need to use all the tools covered in this book. It all depends on the nature and scope of the project you are tackling.

Before moving on to the Measure phase, let's review what you have done and why.

Define helps pull things together and starts the process of clarifying what you are trying to do. The Improvement Charter is particularly useful here, but it also helps with some of the 'softer issues' by securing buy-in and commitment from the team members. Do remember, though, this is a 'living document' that evolves as you increase your understanding of the problem being tackled; it will need updating at the end of the Measure and Analyse phases, in particular.

It's vital you recognise the importance of having a clear picture of what you are trying to achieve and a realisation of who the key stakeholders are. They can make or break your project.

Of course, your customers should be the primary focus of attention and you will need to develop the CTQs either in Define or Measure. If you need to determine them in Measure you will almost certainly have to come back to update the SIPOC which is another key output from this phase.

The high level SIPOC provides an ideal framework to develop your understanding of how the process works and to pinpoint where you should be measuring. And by keeping the diagram at a high level, it can stop you getting lost in the detail of the lower level process and its procedures.

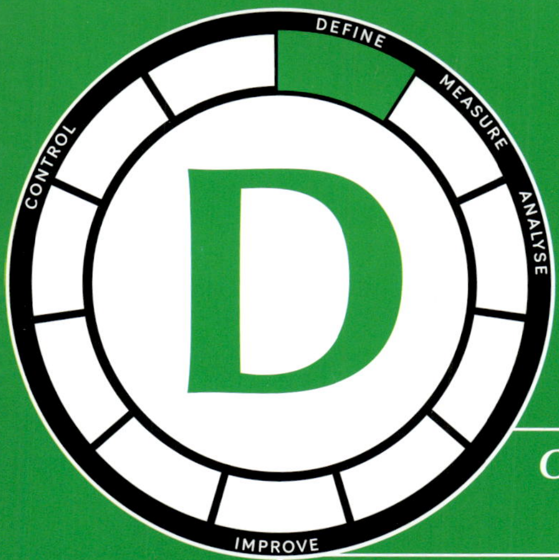

Create Improvement Charter

Agree the CTQs

Develop a SIPOC Diagram

Carry out Stakeholder Analysis

Write an Elevator Speech

Assess Risks

Create the Project Storyboard

Develop the Communications Plan

Step 2 – Understand the current situation

What's this step all about?

In simple terms, it's about how the work gets done and how well it gets done. To understand the current situation, it's important to know what the process looks like and how it's performing. You need to understand what's meant to happen, and why. And it will help you to know how your process links to your customer. What does the bigger picture of the process look like?

Naturally, it's essential to know the current performance – this becomes your baseline, but it will also be helpful to know what's happened in the past. Remember to measure what's important to the customer, and remember to measure what the customer sees. Gathering this information can help focus your improvement efforts and prevent you going off in the wrong direction. And using Control Charts will help you make better sense of the data.

The key outputs

- Confirm the CTQs, if not already agreed
- An updated SIPOC, where necessary
- A current state Deployment Flow-chart or Value Stream Map
- Agreed output measures (the Ys)
- Ideally, agreed input and in-process measures (the Xs), though these might be determined in the Analyse phase
- An agreed Data Collection Plan
- SPC Control Charts
- A baseline measure of performance possibly using Process Sigma
- An updated Improvement Charter
- An updated Storyboard
- An updated Communications Plan

Key questions before moving on

- Have we reviewed and confirmed the CTQs?
- How well does the process flow?
- What's happened in the past? And what's meant to happen now?
- Have we carried out a 'Process Stapling' exercise?
  What really happens now?
- And what do we do when we see the symptoms of the problem?
- Where in the process do the symptoms of the problem appear?
  And when?
- Have we put appropriate measures in place?
- What is the state of our process?
- Have we identified both the Y and X measures?
- What are the measures showing in terms of the Seven Wastes?
- Is our Data Collection Plan sound?
- Is our data appropriately segmented?
- Are the operational definitions free from ambiguity?
- Who is involved? Who isn't? Who else needs to be?
- Have we updated the Improvement Charter?
- Who should we be communicating with now?
  And what should we be telling them?

Key tools for this step

A painless way to find out what really happens in the process and make the pieces fit more effectively…

Process Stapling

One way of really understanding the process is 'Process Stapling'. Very simply, this means taking a customer order, for example, and literally walking it through the entire process.

No matter where it goes, you go too, and in doing so, you will start to see what really happens. Who does what and why. How they do it. Where they do it; and when.

In carrying out this exercise, you will also begin to understand how much travel and movement is involved in the process, enabling you to create a Spaghetti Diagram.

And, of course, the Process Stapling exercise will enable you to spot the frustrations in the process; the inconsistencies and the 'why on earth do we do this?' activities. And, in doing this you will also spot the steps that add value and those that don't.

Typically, only 10–15% of the steps in a process add value, and more often than not, these steps represent as little as 1% of the total process time. Just think about all the delays and 'transport time' in your own processes.

Carrying out a Process Stapling exercise with a small team of people can be an ideal first step before developing a Flow-chart or Value Stream Map.

Taking Process Stapling to the customer

As your understanding of the process increases, you are likely to find real value in extending the Process Stapling concept to your customers. How does your process and its output link to your customer's process? What does their process look like?

And how can you generate improvements in your process that will really add value to the customer and make an impact that delights them?

Spaghetti Diagram

This diagram provides a picture of what's happening in the process. It can track the movement of the 'thing' or 'things' going through the process, and/or the people carrying out the work.

And it can provide some real surprises about how much movement there is. This technique helps surface waste and provides a very visual catalyst to help stimulate change.

Process Stapling links closely to this technique. When done in concert, it can lead to a reduction not only in wasted movement, but in other Non-Value-Add steps, too.

By the way, you may well have used this technique at home! If you have installed a new kitchen you'll know the importance of the triangle formed by the sink, cooker and fridge. So much time can be wasted by unnecessary travel time. Siting the relevant people and equipment together is often a relatively simple way of reducing waste and cycle time.

Don't forgetti the spaghetti!

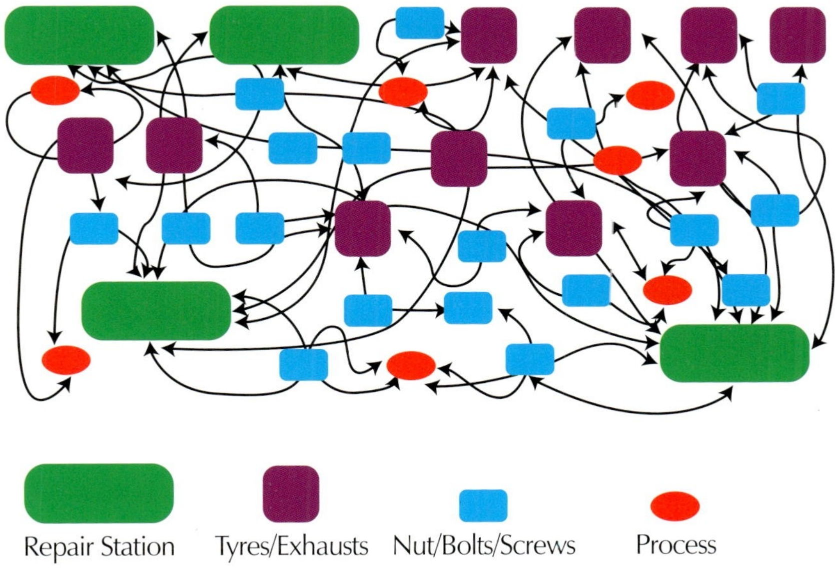

Flow-charts and Process Maps

"If a picture paints a thousand words, then so does a Flow-chart!" It's simply a picture or map of the process... of the workflow

Developing the Flow-chart or Process Map can help you understand how the work gets done, and see if a process looks complicated.

It can highlight the internal and external customer/supplier relationships or 'interfaces,' and help you determine the input and in-process measures you need.

And it can provide a useful framework that prompts questions.

The first step is to develop a high-level or SIPOC Process Map. By looking at a process from a 'big picture' perspective, you can better evaluate customer needs and supplier inputs, and determine initial measurement objectives.

Next, you need to look in more detail at the sub-process defined in the SIPOC map. The sub-processes map provides specifics on the process flow that you can then analyse using several useful techniques.

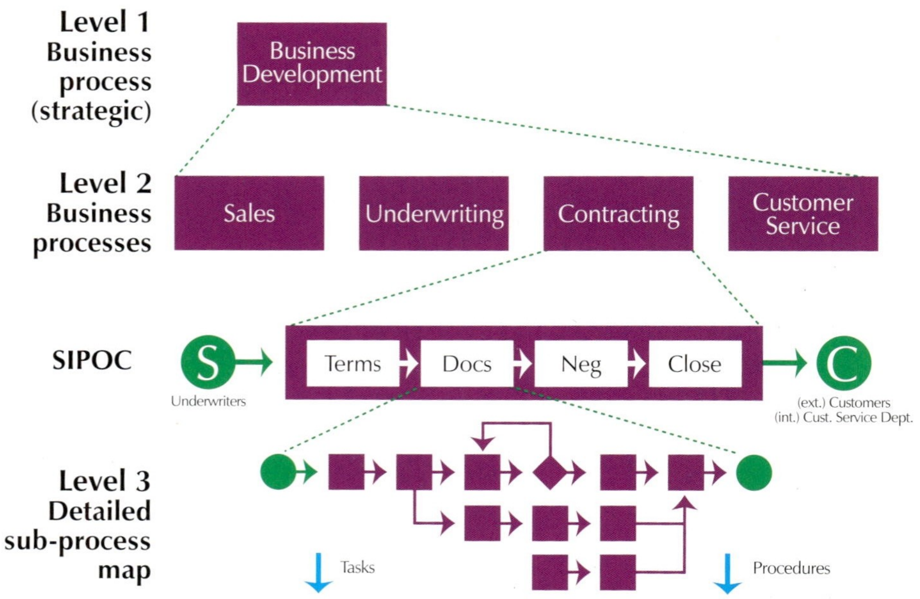

Continue to keep it simple

There are a number of different types of Flow-chart or Process Map; some are complex. In the context of the improvement journey, keep it simple!

Use just one or two Flow-chart 'conventions,' the square box and possibly the diamond:

an activity

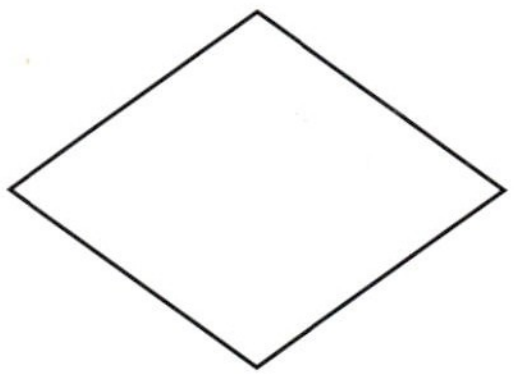

a decision point

Before you begin, make sure you have an agreed objective for the process that reflects the CTQs. In developing a Flow-chart, involve all the people who work in the process, and use Post-its. One Post-it for each step in the process.

Using Post-its makes it very simple to move things around. And almost certainly you will want to, because, undoubtedly, there will be different perceptions on how the process works.

It's also likely to be more complex than you think it is.

The Deployment Flow-chart is a very effective form of Process Map, and one that helps you identify the key process variables and the measures needed. Most problems will occur at the interfaces between two people or departments, for example, and you are sure to need measures here to help monitor performance.

Carrying out a Process Stapling exercise and developing the Flow-chart will also make it easier for you to challenge whether steps in the process add value for the customer. There are three basic requirements to test this:

Testing for customer Value-Add...

Testing for Value-Add (must pass all three tests)

- The customer is prepared to pay for it
- The step must either change the product or service in some way, or be an essential prerequisite
- The step must be actioned 'right first time'

Once identified, many Non-Value-Added tasks can be eliminated by process redesign. Some Non-Value-Added tasks will remain necessary for regulatory or safety/health/environmental considerations. These are called 'essential Non-Value-Add'. The key objective with these tasks is to ensure the process is designed to carry them out as quickly and efficiently as possible.

The moment of truth

The Deployment Flow-chart will also make it easier to spot the 'Moments of Truth' – those touch points with the customer, as well as highlight how your colleagues depend on you to be effective in your way of working.

The difference between the unit time and the cycle time is dead time from a customer perspective

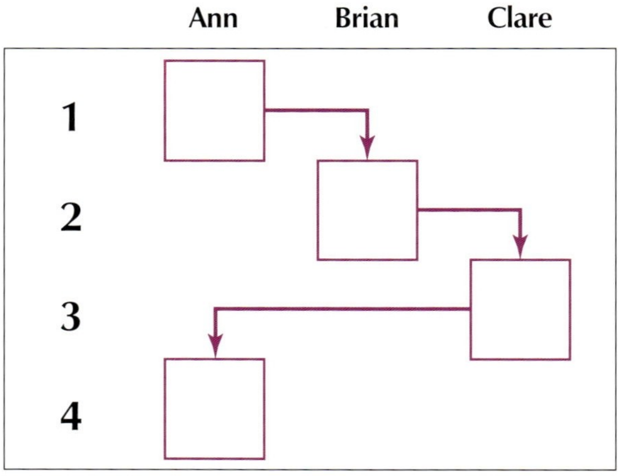

Ann produces something for Brian, and so on. Each time someone else or another area is involved, the chart moves horizontally and down.

You might also include computer systems in your 'cast of characters'.

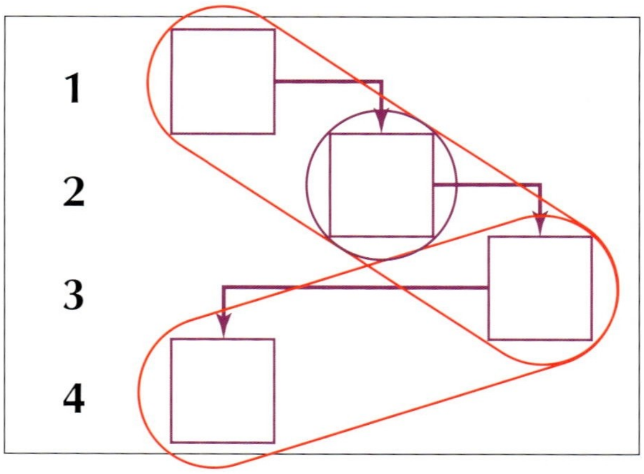

When the chart moves horizontally, there is a customer/supplier relationship. Are the requirements clear and how well are they being met? Measurement can help identify performance and opportunities for improvement. You might measure the number of times requirements are not met and the reasons why, for example.

Unit time
10 mins
2 mins
30 mins
18 mins
1 Hour

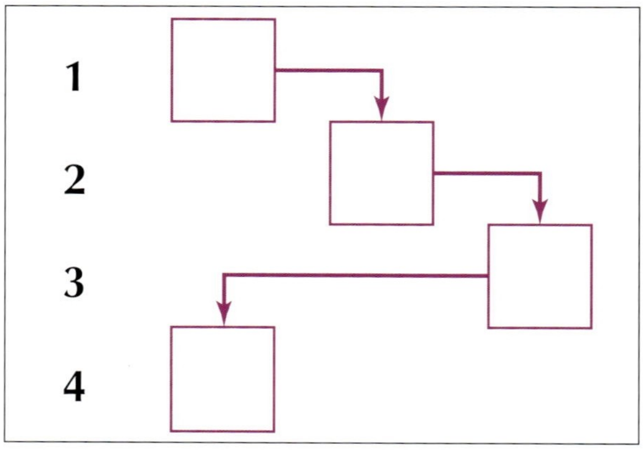

Measuring 'time' can highlight other improvement opportunities. How long does each step take? Why?
Here you are simply measuring 'unit time'. In itself this could prompt some interesting questions, but it's really more helpful to view the bigger picture, by also looking at the elapsed or cycle time.

Unit time	Cycle time
10 mins	10 mins
2 mins	2 days
30 mins	3 days
18 mins	4 days
1 Hour	**4 days**

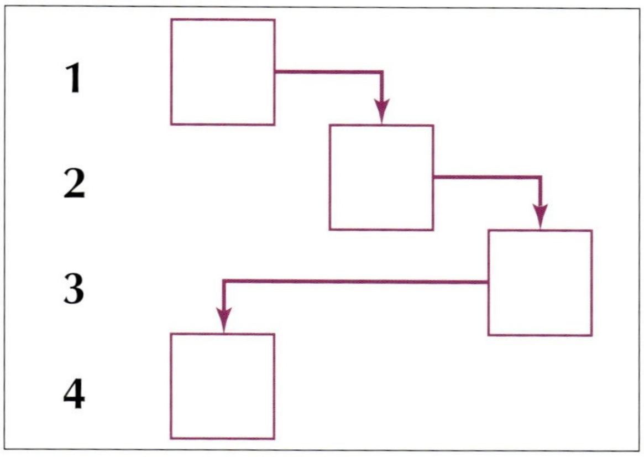

By building in the 'cycle time,' you can identify bottlenecks and 'dead time'. Does step number two add value to the customer? Certainly it's causing a bottleneck. How can you take Brian out of the process? Could Ann or Clare do that work?
If they can, the cycle time is potentially halved.
There are clear links here to the Theory of Constraints and Pull Production.

Ideally, your Deployment Flow-chart will include the external customer, since the important thing is to recognise and understand the 'whole process' or 'system' and to spot the 'Moments of Truth'.

In order to challenge and improve processes, you should continually question each part of the process.

Below are some typical questions that will be prompted by a Flow-charting exercise:

- Who are the customers who have expectations of the process?
- Why is the process done? What is its purpose, does everyone involved understand this?
- What are the Value-Add and Non-Value-Add steps?
- How can I carry out essential Non-Value-Added steps using minimal resource?
- What are the critical success factors – the things you must do well?
- Why is the process done when it is done?
- Why are tasks in the process carried out in that order? Are all the steps involved in the process necessary? Do they add value to the customer?
- Why is the process carried out by that person/those people?
- What measurement is in place that will assess performance and identify possible improvement opportunities? Think in particular of how you might identify and measure those parts of the process which are repetitive and important to ensuring the process conforms to requirements.
- What is the cycle time involved in the process? Why is the cycle time longer than the unit time?
- What might be the barriers which prevent the supplier from producing a quality output?
- If decisions need to be made as part of the process, are the criteria which will be used to make the decisions understood by everyone involved?
  Are the decisions adequately communicated? And are the authority limits appropriate?
- How are problems which occur in the process currently dealt with?
- What are the most common mistakes which occur in the process? What impact do they have on the customers?
- Where have improvements already been tried in the process? What was the outcome?

Whichever questions you ask, don't forget to keep asking "why?"

"A Flow-chart might also prompt a thousand questions..."

Keep asking "why?"

Value Stream Map

The Value Stream Map provides an alternative to the Deployment Flow-chart as a way of looking at how the work gets done.

The Value Stream

The Value Stream sets out all of the actions, both value creating and Non-Value creating, that bring a product from concept to launch, and from order to delivery. These include actions to process information from the customer, and actions to transform the product on its way to the customer. It's nicely summarised in this 1978 quotation from Taiichi Ohno:

> *"All we are doing is looking at a time line from the moment the customer gives us an order to the point when we collect the cash. And we are reducing that time line by removing the Non-Value-Added wastes"*

The link to Process Stapling & SIPOC

As we have already seen in the DMAIC cycle, Process Stapling is a good first step in developing Process Maps. It's also an ideal way to help you create a Value Stream Map. It's a simple diagram that can be drawn at quite a high level and is very similar to a SIPOC Diagram. Ideally it will include a picture of where the various activities are actioned; and will show both the process flow, and the flow of information.

A current state map in service

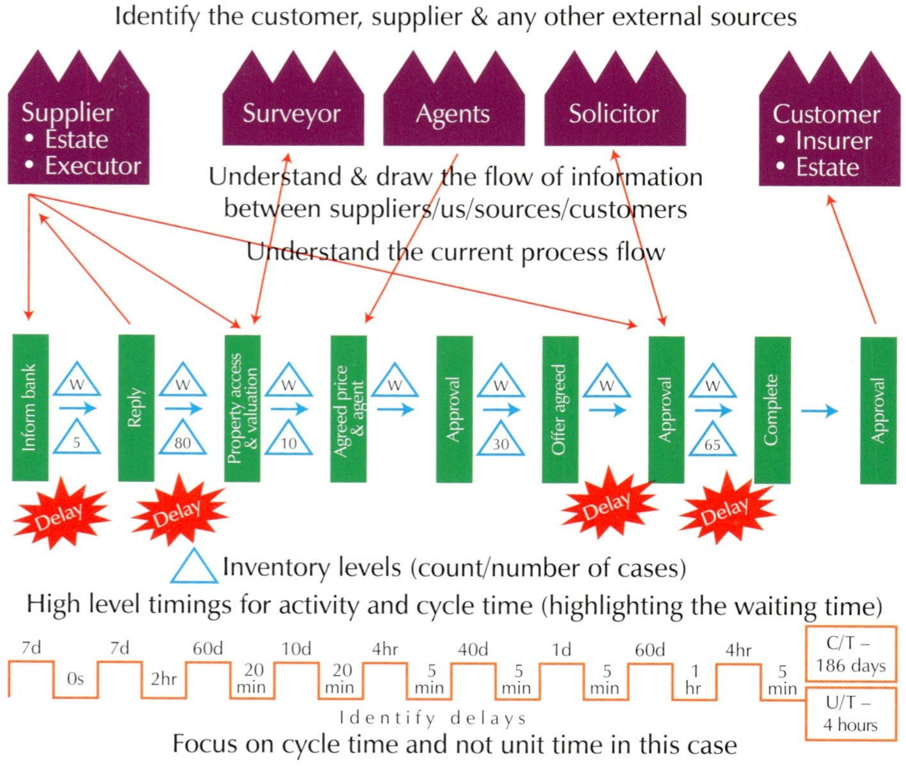

Data boxes

Once you have the current state picture, you need to incorporate some data boxes. These capture a number of variables, including, for example, activity and cycle time, and changeover time. Inventory, or work in progress is picked up in the separate triangles. It's a snapshot at a point in time – and it doesn't matter, for example, whether people feel the inventory isn't usually that high. For whatever reason, it is right now, so why might that be?

The key is to see both the Non-Value-Added activities, as well as the bottlenecks and identify how things can be improved. A future state map shows how the process could be undertaken to achieve a higher level of performance at some future point.

Achieving it may be harder, and, again, could result in the need for a DMAIC project. Of course, once it is achieved, it becomes the current state map, and with continuous improvement in mind, you need to develop a new future state picture.

Value Stream Maps follow a product's path from order to delivery to determine current conditions. They can include a picture of the actual working layout in the office or factory to highlight the impact of transport time, for example.

How to use Value Stream Mapping

The following notes provide a step by step approach and include some of the mapping symbols you are likely to need.

1. Identify the product or service you are going to analyse

2. Set up a small team to do the analysis. Between them they should have a knowledge of all steps involved from supplier input to external customer

3. Go to where the action is to watch what is actually happening

4. Working at a reasonably high level, draw up a Process Map of the material/product flow in the whole value stream as you watch and walk through. Use a sheet of paper and pencils and start at the customer end working backwards. Process Stapling can help you generate that picture. As well as material and product flow, capture the information flow that causes product or material to move through the process.

Material flow icons

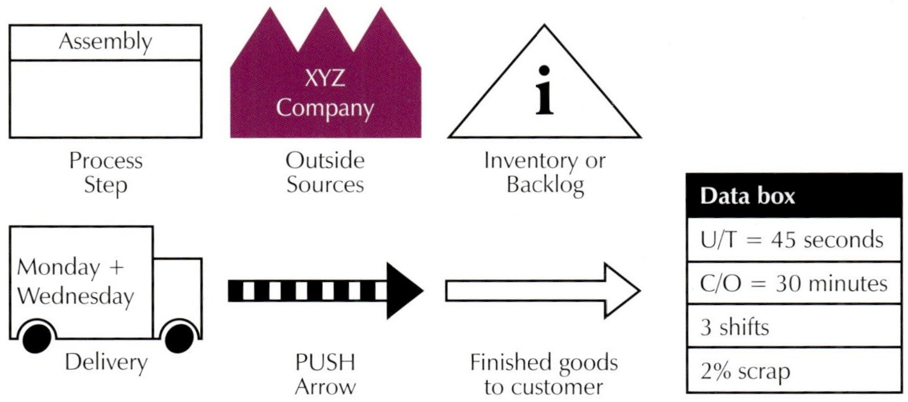

5. Now identify the performance data it would be useful to know. Typically, the information that is useful is:

Unit and Cycle time	Scrap or rework rates
Number of staff/Resources	Batch sizes
Machine uptime	Changeover Time
Working time	Inventory or backlog

6. Now collect the data you need for each step in the process and add it to your map in boxes. For example:

	Check-in desk
Unit time	17 minutes average
Number of staff	1
Working time	2 shifts 8 hours per shift
Re-work rate	Average 3% of passengers with check-in errors
Batch size	Average person per check-in
Machine uptime	99%
Backlog	Average 13 people in queue

7. Now add arrows to show information flows:

Information flow icons

Manual information flow | **Electronic information flow**

But don't forget the average hides things

8. Add overall time line to show average cycle time for an item (i.e. how long it spends in the whole process)

9. Investigate each process step. Is it Value-Added or Non-Value-Added?

10. Stand back and summarise the key measures across the total value chain as follows:

- Total Cycle Time for the item in the process (What is the elapsed time from start to finish?)
- Unit Time. (The actual time spent working on the item). What percentage of cycle time does that represent?
- Value-Added time vs Non-Value-Added time
- Where are the queues, inventory, and backlog? (i.e. the constraints)
- Where is the rework?

Moments of Truth

This concept was developed and popularised by Jan Carlzon [Moments of Truth, Cambridge, MA: Ballinger]. A moment of truth occurs every time a customer comes into contact with a company, be it in person, on the telephone or by post. Indeed, it also applies when they are reading our literature or viewing our advertisements.

They are happening all the time...

Each of these customer 'touch points' provide an opportunity to make or break the organisation, since the customer will either be pleased or displeased with the outcome. Moments of Truth are happening all the time, and we are all responsible for their outcome, for delivering great customer experience.

Who cares wins

Jan Carlzon first introduced this concept as Chief Executive of Scandinavian Air Services (SAS). He pulled all his staff together and told them that the organisation needed to improve by 1000%. Clearly, they would not be able to achieve this overnight, but what he wanted them to do was to improve 1000 things by 1% and to then keep doing it. Importantly, he wanted them to focus on the customer contacts, the Moments of Truth.

So, when somebody booked their airline ticket, or checked in, or boarded the plane, how was the experience? In explaining the concept, he used an example of a passenger pulling down the meal tray on the seat in front of them. If the tray was dirty, what would the customer think? And what would that tell the customer about the maintenance of the plane?!

If we are to achieve the desired state demanded by our customers, we need to understand all of the many Moments of Truth opportunities that exist, and find ways of enhancing the experience for them. Process Stapling and the use of Deployment Flow-charts or Value Stream Maps help identify both the internal and external customer touch points.

Give me the facts…

Getting the measure of your processes

We've already made a number of references to measurement. That shouldn't be surprising – the successful improvement journey needs facts and data.

In fact, measurement is at the heart of our eight-step improvement process. It may well have prompted the project; and it will certainly be needed to understand the current situation. If you are really going to manage by fact, you will need to quantify and verify possible causes. In developing solutions, you will need data to help determine the most effective approach. And following the implementation of your solution, you will need measures in place to help evidence and maintain the gain, and prompt further improvement opportunities.

You get what you measure…

It's generally true that you get what you measure. It's also generally true that measurement can help you manage; you can make decisions based on fact.

Deciding what to measure and how to do it are the keys.

Whatever you do, measure in order to help improvement. Don't measure for measurement's sake.

'SIPOC' provides a framework for your measures

You can anchor your measures to the SIPOC Diagram. You need to measure the **outputs** to the customer to help you understand how well they meet the CTQs. Often their requirements will include 'speed of delivery' and 'accuracy', so you would collect data to measure these '**variables**'

Getting the balance of measures and understanding how they interrelate:

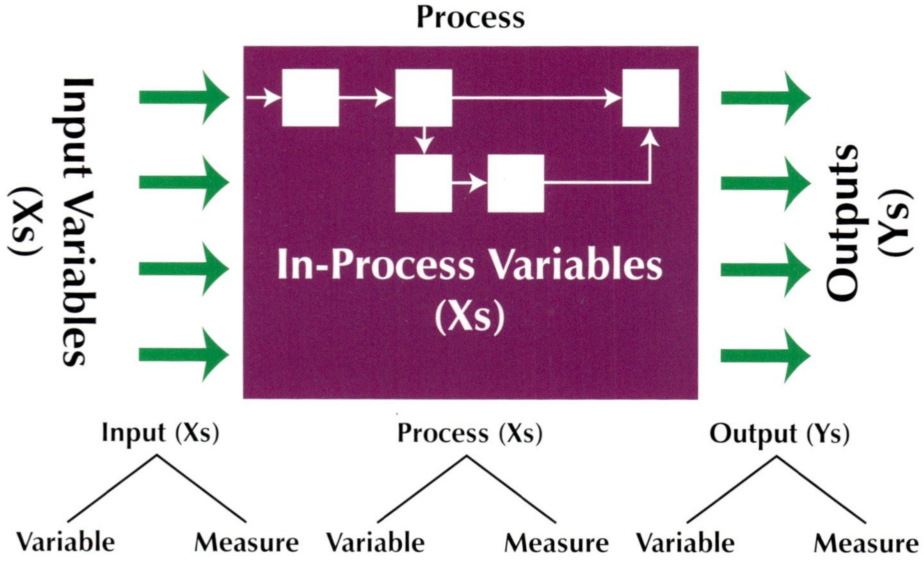

We call them variables simply because the results will vary. If you are measuring the time it takes to provide the customer with a letter, you are likely to find that one case takes two days, another three days and the next, one week, for example. Similarly, some will be produced without any errors; others will be wrongly addressed or not include all the information needed by the customer.

Introducing the concept of variables and variation

In the same way as you need to measure the outputs, you also need to measure the inputs from your suppliers. How well are they meeting your requirements? There are some more variables in the process itself – and you need to measure these, too. You will have a better idea of what to measure here once you have a Process Map or Flow-chart in place.

Importantly, you need a balance of input, in-process and output measures, perhaps one to three measures for each. And you need to recognise that the input and in-process variables will influence the results in your output variables, so your measures should clearly link together.

We need a balance of measures

Really this is all about cause and effect – the **independent** input and in-process variables cause the results in the **dependent** output variables to the customers.

Cause and effect

Start to think of the independent variables (input and in-process) as **'X' measures** and the dependent output variables as **'Y' measures**. You will understand why as we introduce additional tools and techniques such as the Fishbone Diagram and Scatter Diagram.

Xs and Ys, but why?

It's also likely that you will need to segment your data in some way. This might be by different types of customer or product, by the time of the day or month, or by error or complaint type, for example. The earlier you identify these needs the better, otherwise you are likely to find yourself needing additional data when you are trying to analyse the problem.

Finally, remember the importance of customer perception measures. How well do they feel you are performing?

Perceptions are reality to the customer

Data Collection

Data collection is a process that needs to be managed and improved

Data Collection is a process that needs managing and improving just like any other process. It's important to recognise that your measurement and data will be only as good as the process that collects it. There is likely to be enough variation in the operational process itself, without the situation being compounded by variation in the measurement.

Data Collection can be seen as a five step process:

Data Collection step 1

Begin with the outputs

As ever, the first step is to begin with the end in mind. So, agree the objectives and goals for Data Collection ensuring the link to the key outputs. This helps everyone know why the measurement is being undertaken.

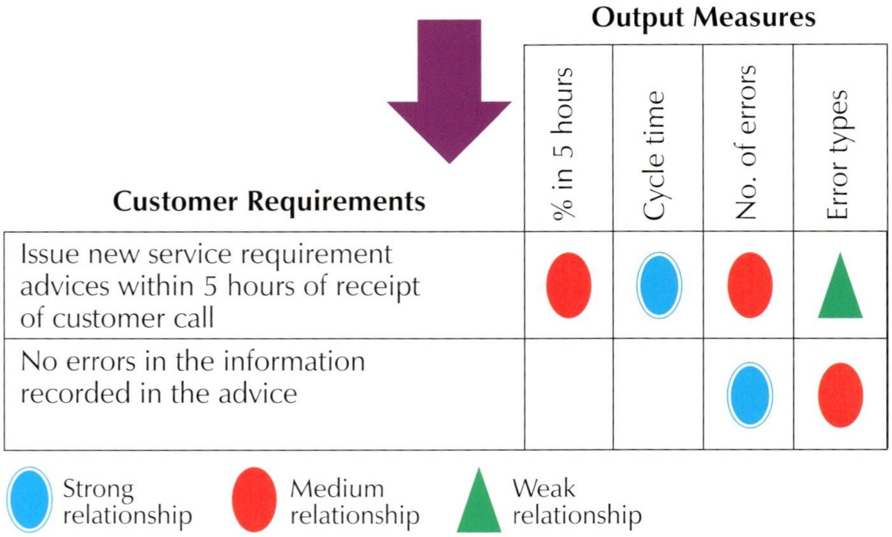

The CTQ customer requirements have been written in a way that is clearly measurable.

The Matrix provides an ideal framework for your measures, and by using the symbols shown, you can check to see if you have an appropriate set. Make sure you have at least one strong measure for each CTQ.

It's important to start with the output measures because you are looking to see how the 'Voice of the Process' matches the 'Voice of the Customer'.

The diagram on the next page illustrates a process that is trying to meet the customer's requirements. The feedback from the customer and the process highlights a gap that needs to be closed, signalling the need for improvement action.

The customer sees what the customer sees

In this example, the average process performance is six days and it's clear that the process isn't capable of meeting the 'five day or less' customer requirement. But even if the average performance had been five days, the process probably would not have been good enough.

Remember that the customer will see each and every case processed and will probably be measuring what they see. If you only report your average performance it can be misleading. Averages and 'percentages in standard' can disguise what's really happening.

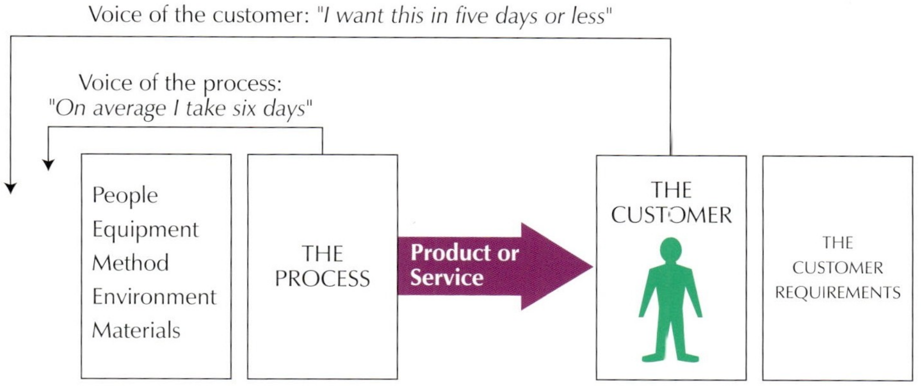

A process that is trying to meet the customer's requirements

So, be careful about what you measure and how you present the Voice of the Process data. It might be that the process performance varies considerably with some cases taking only a day or two whilst others perhaps take as long as 10 or 15 days, for example. An average of five days will not be what the customer sees. That's why cycle time is so important, something that has been reflected in the Output Measures Matrix on page 50.

And just in case you need convincing, I'm sure you will agree with the rail companies when they tell you there's no overcrowding on their trains! On average that is!

Don't hide behind the average

Remember Mr Kipling?

Data Collection step 2

Now you know what you are planning to measure, it's important to provide clear, unambiguous **operational definitions**. These will help ensure everyone understands the 'Who, What, Where, When, and How' of the measurement process and result in consistent data. So, if you are measuring cycle time, for example, when does the clock start and finish? And which clock are you using? Are you measuring in seconds, minutes, or hours? And do you round up or down? Unless issues like this are clear, wide variation in the measurement process will be certain.

Gauge R and R can be done simply

Data Collection step 3

Kipling's serving men will also help you ensure that the ongoing data is both valid and consistent. And you can check this out using Gauge R and R. This is a technique that can be used to assess the Repeatability and Reproducibility of the measuring system. It's a means of checking how much the measurement system is contributing to process variation.

Repeatability is the variation when one operator uses the same system. **Reproducibility** is the variation when different operators use the same system. So, for repeatability, if you measure a batch of cases, then measure the same batch again, will you get the same results? And for reproducibility, would the results be different if someone else measured the same batch?

For a service organisation, if Gauge R and R exceeds 10%, think carefully about improving the measurement system. If it exceeds 25% then change the measurement system. If there are safety or regulatory issues involved, then these rule of thumb guidelines need to be a lot tighter.

In the following example, two people have checked the same batch of cases, though in a random sequence.

From the difference of the two readings, averaged over the number of cases in the batch, the Gauge R and R can be inferred.

The table shows the Gauge R and R is good for total time at 0.42%, but is less accurate though still acceptable for sub-processes. Overall, you should be very pleased with the results, though you might want to see if things can be improved for 'vet form'.

Measure	Timekeeper A	Timekeeper B	Tolerance
Vet form	45	41	9.30%
Add info. to form	90	89	1.12%
Update records	175	177	1.14%
Print agreement	100	95	5.13%
Issue to customer	66	72	8.70%
Total Time	476	474	**0.42%**

A more rigorous approach can be taken using other statistical tools but this is outside the scope of this booklet where our approach is to keep things simple.

Data Collection step 4

Almost certainly, at least some of your data will need to be collected manually. Data Collection Sheets will be needed both to make this as straightforward as possible, and, of course, to help ensure consistency.

These might be as simple as a Check Sheet or Tally Chart. Simply recording 'five bar gate' style, the number of times 'something' occurs.
The Check Sheet picks up the dimension of time and links neatly to Pareto, as the example shows:

A Check Sheet

No.	Characteristic	Day 1	2	3	4	5	6	7	8	9	10	Total
A	Form not signed	II	I	0	I	0	I	I	0	0	I	7
B	No part number	I	0	II	I	I	II	0	0	0	0	7
C	Address missing	𝍸	II	III	II	III	IIII	III	𝍸	III	III	33
D	No cheque attached	I	0	I	I	I	0	I	I	I	I	8
E	Wrong amount	III	IIII	I	III	I	II	III	III	IIII	𝍸	29
Total Errors		**12**	**7**	**7**	**8**	**6**	**9**	**8**	**9**	**8**	**10**	**84**

A Tally Chart

Time (days) to complete 'something'	No. of Readings	Total
3	II	**2**
4	IIII	**4**
5	𝍸 III	**8**
6	𝍸 𝍸 𝍸	**15**
7	𝍸 𝍸 𝍸 𝍸 𝍸 II	**27**
8	𝍸 𝍸 𝍸 IIII	**19**
9	𝍸 𝍸 II	**12**
10	𝍸 𝍸 I	**11**
11	II	**2**
		100

Other options include the Concentration Diagram – a technique that can be applied in the office, but that is usually associated with physical product. Often it is used to identify damage to goods in transit, by recording, for example, where on the product or packaging dents, gouges, and scratches occur. Some of you will have seen its use hiring a car, or in insurance!

These examples show some possible applications:

Expense report form — hire cars and insurance claims

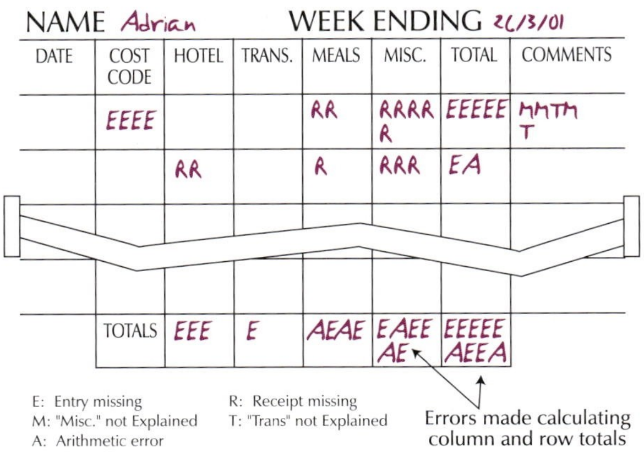

◀ *A blank expenses form has been used to capture details of the number & type of errors, and where on the form they occur.*

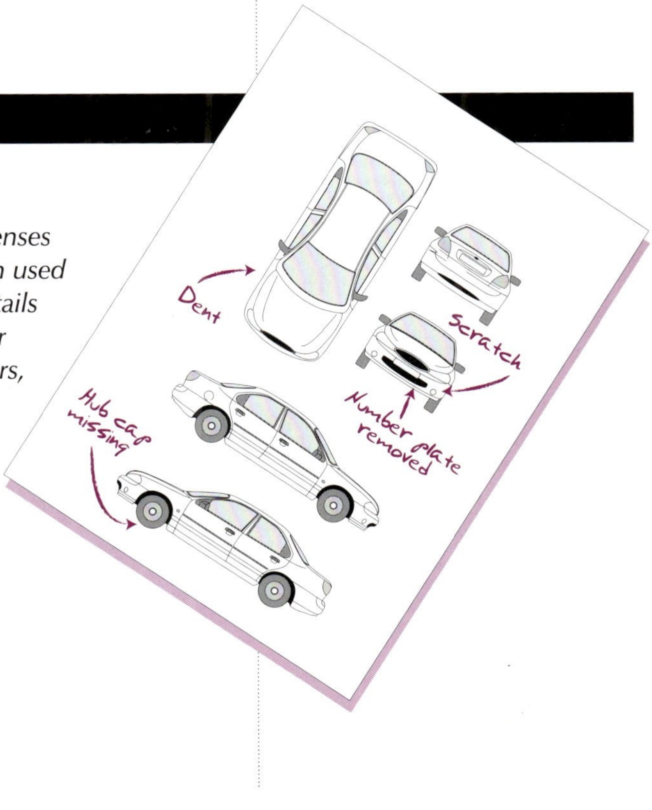

Data Collection step 5

Data Collection is a process

Remembering that Data Collection is a process, carry on collecting the data, identifying ways to improve the approach. If you haven't already done so, you will need to identify and measure the 'upstream variables' that are influencing the output performance of your process, either now, or as part of the Analyse phase.

So, what are the input and in-process X variables, and how can you measure them? You might find it helpful to develop a Y to Xs Matrix:

What are the input & in-process X variables?

Output Measures							What are the input & in-process measures?
% in five hours							
Cycle time							
Number of errors							
Type of errors							

Strong relationship   Medium relationship   Weak relationship

Typical X variables will include volumes of work in, supplier accuracy and timeliness, available resources, and in-process cycle times. How would you measure these and how strong an influence do you feel they are having on the Y measures from your earlier Matrix? Do you have an appropriate set of X measures? Overall, you should review your various X and Y measures in 'Kipling's Data Collection Summary' to help ensure you have an appropriate balance and plan.

A collection of Kipling?

Kipling's Data Collection summary

Type of measure	What? What are we measuring?	Why? Why are we measuring this?	How? How do we collect and record the data?	When? When do we collect the data?	Where? Where in the process?	Who? Who will collect it?
Output						
In-process						
Input						

Sampling

One of the important decisions to make in the collection and analysis of data is whether to look at everything, or take a sample. And if you take a sample, how big does it need to be?

What are you inferring?

Sampling means that you are collecting only a representative selection of the available or potentially available data, before analysing it to draw conclusions about the total data (Statistical Inference).

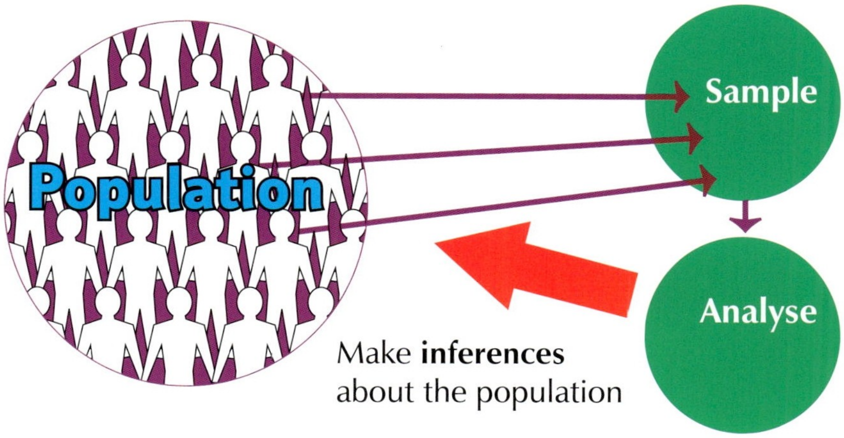

Sampling the vine can prove expensive...

Sampling is used when it is too difficult or expensive to collect and analyse all the data. And sometimes collecting the data destroys it, as with wine tasting, or the testing of sutures, for example. Importantly, valid conclusions can often be drawn from a comparatively small amount of data. For conclusions to be valid, the samples must be representative, so that the data you collect fairly represents all of the data. There should be no systematic differences between the data you collect and the data you don't collect. In other words, every item stands an equal chance of being included.

As ever, understand your customers as part of understanding the segmentation factors

Apart from anything else, that means if you don't understand the segmentation factors involved, you could take an inappropriate sample. There are a whole host of ways for 'bias' to creep into your sample without this mistake.

If you don't understand the segmentation factors of the population, you could take an inappropriate sample

This booklet looks at two types of sampling, process and population.

The purpose of process sampling is to measure, analyse or control the process. Examples include establishing the baseline performance, identifying opportunities for improvement, and ensuring ongoing monitoring and control.

'The sampling process'

There are two broad approaches to process sampling. The first involves taking a regular sample, for example every third or tenth item. This is known as systematic sampling; it is often used for comparatively low volume administrative processes. It can be relatively easy to do, but may introduce bias, if, for example, there is something significant about every third or tenth item. The data links into a X moving R Control Chart.

Systematic sampling from a process

Taking a regular sample, for example every third or tenth item etc. This can be relatively easy to do, but may introduce bias.

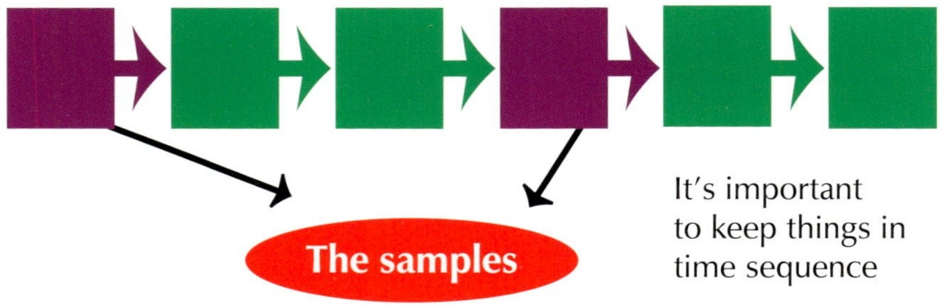

'Look out for bias!'

Sub-group sampling involves taking a regular and random sample of, for example, five items, perhaps every day. It is used with comparatively high volume processes where it is not practical to look at each and every item, or even every tenth or so. The data links neatly with the X bar R Control Chart.

Sub-group sampling from a process

Take a regular and random sample of five items, every hour or two, or every day, for example.

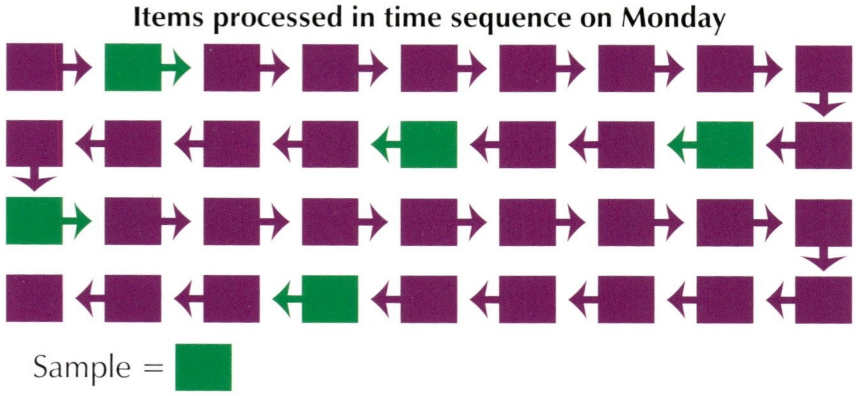

Let's take a look at the population...

As the name suggests, population sampling looks at populations. This could mean a customer base, or a population of something that's already been processed, for example, loan applications. Other examples include voting intentions of particular groups, the buying patterns of potential customers, or the reasons for defaulting on mortgage payments.

So, how do you go about determining the sample size? How large need it be? The flippant answer is "how large can you afford it to be?"

How much can you afford?

Broadly, the larger it is, the more accurate it is. But much will be determined by what you want the data for, how accurate it needs to be, and how much variation there is within the population. If the population were all clones, for example, you would need to sample only one of them!

Let's start by looking at how accurate you need the sample to be. This is determined by precision. Precision is how narrow you want the range to be for your estimate. So, for example, estimate the cycle time within two days, or estimate the 'percent defective' within three percent. The symbol d for 'delta' is used to represent precision in the sample size formulae.

To be precise...

Precision is equal to half the width of a 'confidence interval'. So, if your sample of data shows a mean average of 50 days, you are 95% confident the interval from 48 to 52 days contains the average cycle time. In this example, the width of the confidence interval is four days, and the estimate is within +/- two days.

The usual convention is to work with a 95% confidence level and the formulae are set on that basis

The level of precision will vary according to your requirements. Why do you want the data? What decisions will you be making as a result?

So, for example, imagine your mortgage service team has processed 15,000 'e-loan' enquiries, and you want to determine the average processing time.

Depending on why you need the information, does your estimate have to be within five minutes, or five seconds? If you are determining staffing and budget requirements, you are likely to want the estimate to be pretty accurate.

You might be surprised to see how the sample size changes according to this requirement. The formula needed to estimate the average cycle time is:

$$\text{Estimate Average cycle time} \quad n = \left(\frac{2s}{d}\right)^2$$

Where n is the sample size needed, s is the standard deviation, and d is the precision

Let's work through an example, where you want to estimate the average processing time within one minute. To estimate the sample size, you need to know the standard deviation. You need to have some idea of the amount of variation in the data because as the variability increases, the necessary sample size increases.

But if you haven't sampled anything yet, how can you know the standard deviation? It may be that you already have some historical data on this, or could use Control Chart data from a similar process. If not, you might need to collect a small sample, perhaps as few as 25, and calculate the standard deviation first.

Catch 22 is alive and well...

In the example, you have calculated the standard deviation is three minutes. So, plugging the various numbers into the formula, the sample size needed is 36.

$$n = \left(\frac{2 \times 3}{1}\right)^2 = 6^2 = 36$$

The more accurate you need it to be, the larger the sample

That number increases to 144 if the precision is 30 seconds. And to 2304 if the precision changes to 7.5 seconds.

$$n = \left(\frac{2 \times 3}{0.5}\right)^2 = 12^2 = 144$$

$$n = \left(\frac{2 \times 3}{0.125}\right)^2 = 48^2 = 2304$$

The formula changes to estimate proportions:

Estimating proportions

It's important to realise that sample sizes change significantly according to the p value

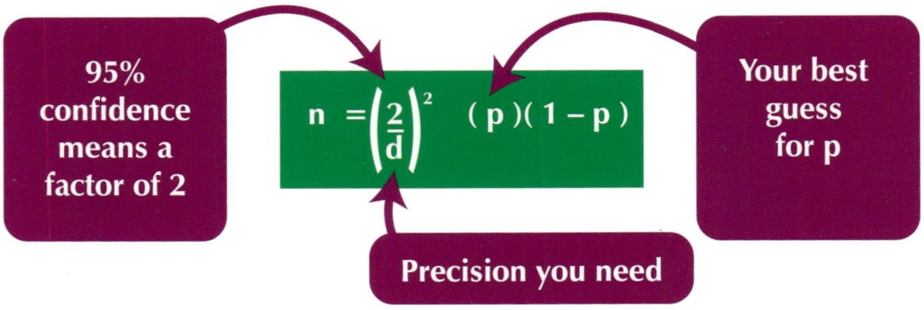

What's your best guess of p?

As before, the usual convention is to work with a 95% confidence level. The tricky bit is to determine your best guess for (p), though this may not really be as hard as it sounds. There may be similar processes already in place, or you may already have a pretty good idea of the 'proportion defective'. The largest sample size occurs when p = 0.5 or 50%, so if you have no idea what (p) might be, assume it is 0.5. The worst outcome is simply a larger than necessary sample. Incidentally, the proportion defective is a phrase that doesn't simply describe defects! It might relate to the proportion of customers who are likely to purchase a new product or service, for example.

There may be nothing wrong with the proportion defective

Again, let's work through an example. What is the sample size required to estimate the defect rate in a process, with 95% confidence, when you expect it to be around '10% defective', and where you want the estimate to be within 3%?

The answer with a 3% precision

$$n = \left(\frac{2}{d}\right)^2 (p)(1-p)$$

$$n = \left(\frac{2}{0.03}\right)^2 (0.10)(1-0.10)$$

$$n = 4444.4 \times 0.10 \times 0.90 = 400$$

The sample size changes to 3600 if you want the estimate to be within ±1%.

Again, you can see the impact of precision

The answer gets a lot bigger with precision at 1%

$$n = \left(\frac{2}{d}\right)^2 (p)(1-p)$$

$$n = \left(\frac{2}{0.01}\right)^2 (0.10)(1-0.10)$$

$$n = 40000 \times 0.10 \times 0.90 = 3600$$

The sample size formulas assume the sample size (n) is small relative to the population (N). If you are sampling more than 5% of the population, and n/N is greater than 0.05, this may be more than you need, and you can adjust the sample size with the 'Finite Population' formula:

Keeping a check and balance...

Sampling from a limited (finite) population

$$n_{finite} = \frac{n}{1 + n/N}$$

Let's see how this reduces the sample size of 2304 that we calculated at the top of page 58. Remember the population size in this example was 15,000. As you can see, we can reduce the sample to just under 2000, as shown below:

You may not need as many as you thought

$$n_{finite} = \frac{2304}{1 + 2304/15{,}000} = \frac{2304}{1.1536} = 1997$$

You may have worked out the sample size needed for the precision you would like, but how big a sample can you afford to look at? If it's less than the sample size should be, what will the affordable sample provide in terms of precision? And, will that be precise enough? By moving our formula around we can see:

It's a question of how much you can afford

Calculating precision from the affordable sample size

- For an average within ± d units

$$d = \frac{2s}{\sqrt{n}}$$

- A proportion within ± d%

$$d = 2 \times \sqrt{\frac{(p)(1-p)}{n}}$$

This booklet has provided an overview of sampling and the formulae needed to determine sample sizes. Hopefully, it's enabled you to appreciate that valid conclusions can be drawn from comparatively small samples, but that in order for your sample to avoid bias, it must be representative.

SPC – Control Charts

Control Charts – a variation in understanding

The most effective way to understand the 'Voice of the Process' is to use Statistical Process Control – SPC.

Traditionally, SPC has been used in manufacturing, and most examples of its use are from the motor or chemical industries. Its potential in the service industry, and in administrative areas generally is, however, enormous.

So how does it work? Like most things, SPC works only if management behaviour and actions support it. That support starts with the acceptance that 'variation' exists in everything. There is variation in our heights, in the colour green, in the number of words in the sentences of this booklet and in the time different people take to read it. Things are not exactly the same, even if they appear to be.

Importantly, there are two types of variation: sometimes known as 'common cause' or natural variation, and 'special cause'. SPC can help you to identify variation and which type it is. Natural variation is just that – natural. You should expect it. You should not be surprised by it, and you should not react to individual examples of it. If you do, it's likely to make things worse and increase the amount of variation. Deming described this as 'tampering'.

When a process exhibits only natural variation, it is said to be in 'statistical control'. It is 'stable' and predictable, but that doesn't necessarily mean the results from the process are good. They might be very poor. But if the process is 'stable', it can be reviewed as a whole with improvement in mind.

This can probably be best demonstrated by a simple experiment that you can try in the privacy of your own home, or perhaps at work with some colleagues. The first step is to write down the letter 'a' five times.

That in itself can form the basis for an interesting discussion on giving clear instructions; in ensuring that the requirements are understood. Some of you will have written across the page; some down the page. Some will have used upper case; others lower case. One or two of you may even have written 'the letter 'a' five times'. Either way, look at your own letters; are they the same?

Almost certainly they will not be; they will probably all be slightly different. The difference will be 'common cause' variation, and the process will be in 'statistical control'. If you repeated the exercise you could expect to see the same sort of variation. To improve the process, you could automate it or introduce the use of a template, for example.

But what might happen if you 'tampered' with the process by reacting to an individual example of 'common cause' variation? By trying the other hand, for example. The result is likely to show increased variation.

Tampering can also take the form of pointless discussion. Do you see reports that are 'simply' a page of numbers that you are expected to make sense of; perhaps even make decisions on? Sales activity is usually a good example. "This week's figures were better than last week's, but not as good as the week before that," or "Well it rained last Thursday, but the team did a great job this week!" Do you hear this type of comment in your business unit?

I'll be surprised if the answer is 'no'. And yet probably the differences in the weekly figures will be natural variation in the process. Using SPC will confirm this or not, and can help make sense out of a mass, or even a mess of figures.

A run chart helps present data over time, and is simple to construct

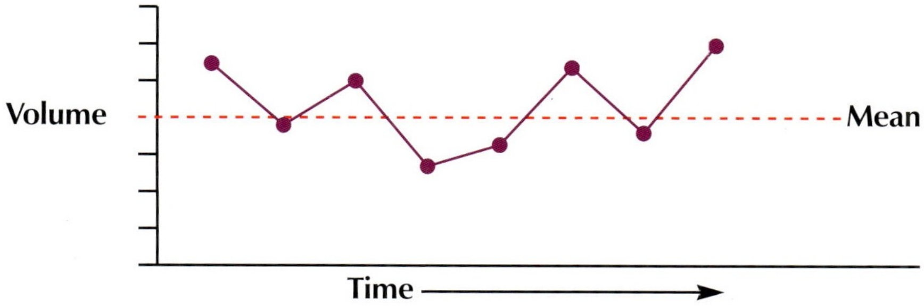

You can start by presenting the data more visually as a run chart.

This makes it easier to spot any trends, but in itself doesn't tell you whether the variation is special or natural. You need a 'Control Chart' to do that.

Using the results from the process, you can calculate the 'mean' or average, and the 'control limits'. A standard formula produces the 'upper control limit', and the 'lower control limit'. Essentially, these are plus and minus three 'standard deviations' from the mean, but please do not worry about the maths. The example below shows a process that is exhibiting variation.

Control Chart

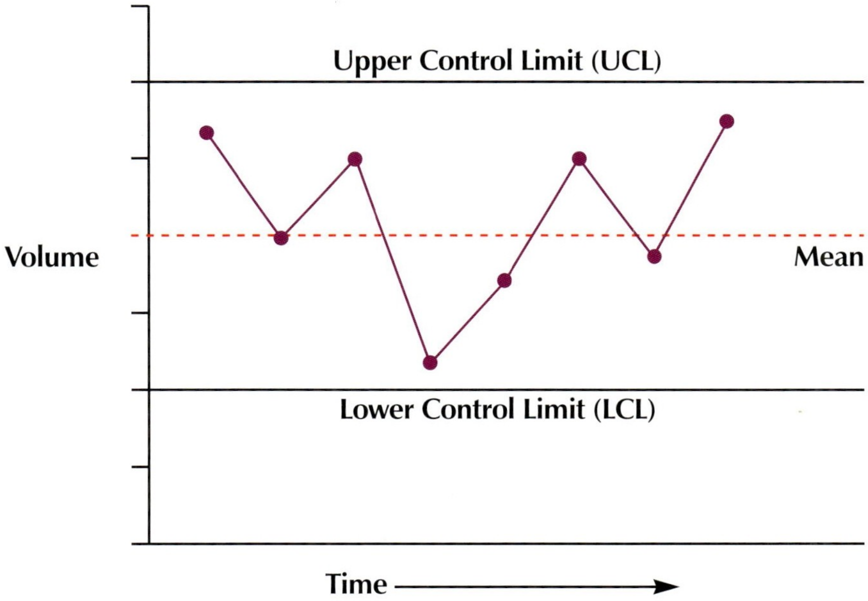

A process that is exhibiting natural variation.

A stable and predictable process isn't necessarily a good one

But it is all natural variation. We know that, because we can use the 'rules' of SPC to distinguish the type of variation. At this stage, it is easiest to work on the lines that if the variation is inside the control limits, then it is natural variation. That will not always be the case, but I'll explain the other rules a little later on.

If the process is exhibiting only natural variation, then it can be described as being in 'statistical control'. It is 'stable'. So what does that mean? Firstly, let me underline what it doesn't mean! It doesn't mean the results are necessarily good; indeed, there might be a very wide gap between the Voice of the Process and the Voice of the Customer.

But the chart is giving you some very important messages. It's telling you that the process results are predictable and you will continue to get results that display variation within the control limits. So don't be surprised, and don't react to individual data items. As far as the process is concerned, these numbers are all the same. Importantly, because the process is stable, you can safely undertake a review of the whole process to find improvement opportunities.

Special causes need investigation

Where improvement action has been taken, the chart should be updated to show the details. It's very important that charts are used in this way to provide a living record of what's happening. A 'clean' Control Chart probably isn't being used properly.

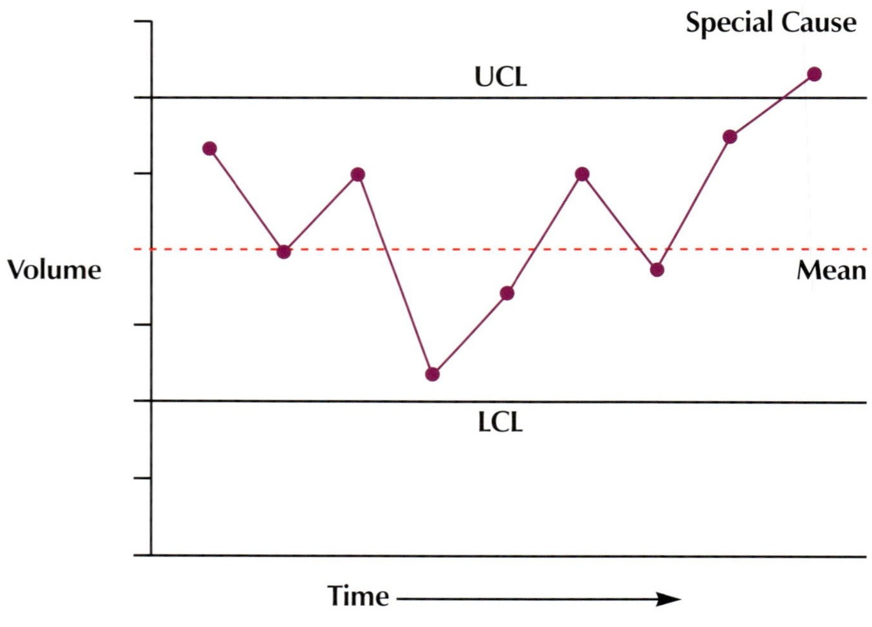

Control Chart – a special cause appears outside the control limits.

So how do you identify special cause variation? And what do you do when you find it? Special causes are identified in a number of ways. The most obvious is when a data item appears outside the control limits.

When that happens, you need to find the 'root cause' and take one of three actions. The options are to remove the data item from the chart, or to take action that either prevents the special cause from occurring again or builds it into the process if it is something good. Not all special causes are bad!

You might remove the special cause from your data when you find it belongs to a different process. Let me explain. In this example, the SPC chart might be measuring the time taken to produce something or to process claims in an insurance company, for example. The process appears to be stable, with an average time of x days, when a special cause appears. This is for a claim that has taken y days, but when you look at the case in detail, you find it is a particular type of claim that always has to be referred to the actuarial department. In fact, it is a member of a 'different population', a different type of claim and a different process. What you need to do is set up a separate chart for this type of claim so that you can understand that process and find ways to improve it.

Special causes can be identified in a number of other ways. A run of seven points all above or all below the 'mean', or all increasing or decreasing. Any unusual patterns or trends within the control limits, or the number of points within the 'middle third' of the region between the control limits differing markedly from two thirds of the total number of points.

Process improvement comes down to two words: 'Reduce Variation!'

A special cause that you will be particularly pleased to see will be the proof that a change in the process has been successful. In the next chart you can see a process that was in statistical control.

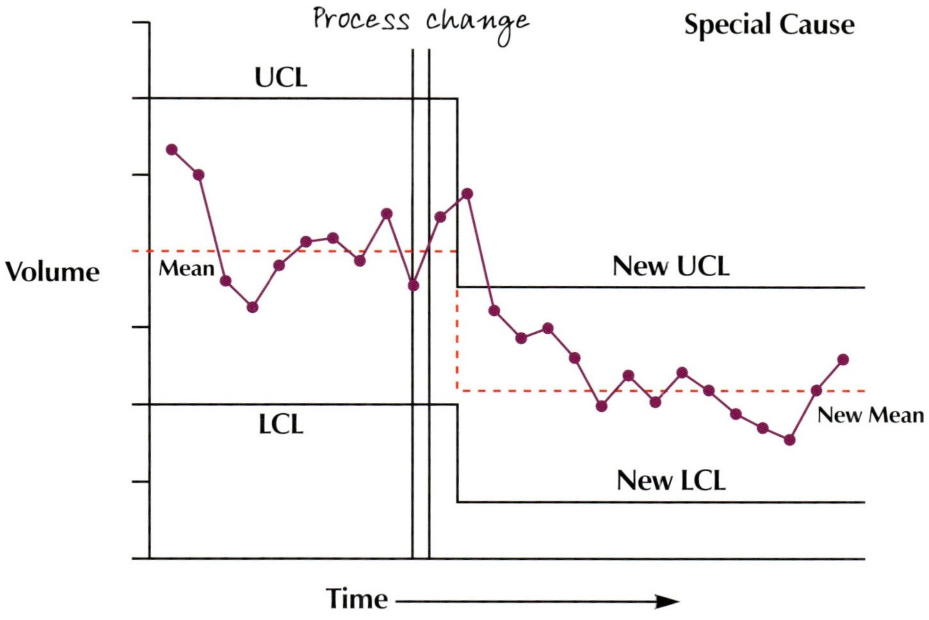

New control limits set after a process review and improvement action.

A process review has been carried out and improvement action taken. The subsequent results identify a special cause, with seven consecutive points below the mean. The improvement has worked, and the Control Chart has given us the evidence. Importantly, you can now recalculate the control limits, and start down a track that will perhaps highlight new special causes to be actioned. Ideally, you will do this once you have 20 data points from the beginning of the special cause, though it can be done with less.

Deming's message to managers came down to two words; "Reduce variation." As you can see, that's exactly what you are trying to do. Reduce variation and bring the control limits ever closer together.

Using Control Charts can show you a number of important things that enable you to make more effective decisions. In particular, they can help you determine the state of your processes, and transform your operational meetings.

What state are your processes in?

In an '**ideal**' state, the process is in statistical control and meets the customer's requirements. If you use a traffic light system at your operations meetings, then this is a green light – no discussion is needed about why this week's numbers differ from last week's. By continuing to use the Control Chart, you can monitor the process and make sure it stays ideal. Of course, you might also be thinking about how to improve on ideal, in the sense of delighting the customer, for example, or reducing the costs associated with the process.

A '**threshold**' state describes a process that is in statistical control, but that doesn't meet the customer specifications. This is an orange light – what action is being taken or planned to bring the process into an ideal state?

By continuing to use the Control Chart, you can monitor the effectiveness of your improvement effort and provide evidence that it has worked.

When a process is '**on the brink**', it's meeting the customer's requirements, but is not in statistical control. In other words, it has special causes and is not predictable. At any moment it may slip into chaos.

'**Chaos**' indicates a process that is not in statistical control and that doesn't meet the customer specifications.

When a process is in a state of chaos or on the brink, it's a red light situation. The continuing use of the Control Chart can help you monitor the removal of special causes and the eventual improvement of the process. It's essential to remove these special causes from the process before you begin to change it, because they will otherwise frustrate your improvement efforts.

There are a number of different SPC charts, but broadly they are the same. 'Variable' charts, for example, can measure time, volumes or amounts of money. 'Attribute' charts will measure whether a particular characteristic is present, or if something is right or wrong. So you can use Control Charts to monitor cycle times or error types, for example. Each type of chart has its own standard formula to calculate the control limits, but the rules for identifying common and special cause variation are broadly consistent.

'Single readings may be the answer…'

The formulae for the variable charts you are likely to use most often, the X moving R and the X bar R charts, are set out on the next page. These charts are ideal for measuring cycle time performance. The X moving R chart is sometimes referred to as an 'Individuals' chart and can also be used to measure volumes of items and activities, or to present attribute data such as 'proportions' or 'percentages' by treating them as 'single readings'.

As you become more experienced in using SPC, you can consider a wider range of chart options.

With the two variable charts, control limits are calculated both for the X and the R values. The resulting two charts should be interpreted together, and if either one shows a special cause, then the process is out of control.

'Two charts in one...'

The X moving R chart

$$UCL_X = \bar{X} + (A_2\bar{R}) \qquad LCL_X = \bar{X} - (A_2\bar{R})$$

A_2 is one of a number of constant values used in calculating control limits. If the moving range is determined by looking at each pair of Xs, then A_2 will always be 2.66

The formula for the Moving Range part of the chart is:

$$UCL_R = D_4\bar{R} \qquad LCL_R = D_3\bar{R}$$

D_4 is another of the constants used. Its value for the X moving R chart is 3.267
D_3 has no value for this chart, and the LCL_R will always be zero

In determining the moving range values, for the X moving R chart, each value of X is used twice. If we are to apply the 'run of seven rule', we need seven independent moving range values, which in effect means 14 successive R values. As a result, a number of organisations tend not to plot the moving R values, but concentrate instead on the values of X.

'A run of 14 is needed here'

With the X bar R chart it is essential that both the X and R values are plotted. The X bar chart shows the variation between the samples; the Range chart highlights the variation within the samples that might otherwise be hidden by the averaging of the sample values in the X part of the chart.

The X bar R chart

$$UCL_{\bar{X}} = \bar{\bar{X}} + (A_2\bar{R}) \qquad LCL_{\bar{X}} = \bar{\bar{X}} - (A_2\bar{R})$$

The value of A_2 varies according to sample size. A sample size of 5 is frequently used, and in this event A_2 will be 0.577

The formula for the Range part of the chart is:

$$UCL_R = D_4\bar{R} \qquad LCL_R = D_3\bar{R}$$

With a sample size of 5, D_4 is 2.114 and D_3 is zero again

Control charts provide a key technique in the analysis, control, and improvement of processes, but as Deming said, "The use of Control Charts should start with management, not on the shop floor." Management must understand variation and behave as though they understand it.

Where to begin...

Capability

Earlier, we mentioned that a process in statistical control might not be a good process. It's predictable, but may not be meeting the customer CTQs.

Building on your 'state of the process' descriptions, you can use two capability indices to help assess performance – they are relevant only when the process is in control. The first looks at the variation in the process compared to the specification of the CTQs. This is the Cp index – it's a little like gauging whether or not you can get your car through a gap.

Imagine the width of the control limits in your Control Chart is represented by the width of the car in the illustration. Is it possible to drive it through the arch that is representing the width of the customer specification limits?

Are you sure you can get through that gap?

Is the process 'Inherently Capable'?

The width of car represents the control limits for 'the process'

Careful drivers only

The process is 'Inherently Capable' but only if it's 'centred'

In the example, you can see that it is possible, but only just! You need to be driving very carefully – the process needs to be 'centred'. In other words, you need to ensure that the mean of the Control Chart is lined up with the mid-point of the customer specification. The Cp index tells us how many times the car can – in theory – fit inside the arch; in the example, it only just fits once, so the Cp value will be 1.0.

The second capability index is Cpk and it describes the 'location'. It tells you how well you are driving in practice.

So, how well are we driving?

As you can see, the driving needs some improvement! The Cpk value would be less than the Cp value and if it's less than 1.0 it won't be meeting the CTQ. In process terms, you need to shift the mean by finding a way to improve this 'threshold' process.

How well is it being driven?

As you can see, if the process is off centre then it will not be capable

You need both values to be able to fully assess a process, but the process needs to be in control for these indices to be meaningful.

You'll find that the Cpk value can never be greater than the Cp value. When the process mean is running on the 'nominal', then Cpk and Cp are the same value. The nominal is the mid-point of the customer specification

It's the nominal phenomenal

Improving your processes requires you to increase the Cp value, making sure that as far as possible, the Cpk value remains equal to Cp.

So, how do you calculate these indices? Let's start by remembering that the difference between the upper and lower control limits on your Control Chart covers six standard deviations. The difference between the upper and lower customer specification (USL – LSL) is usually referred to as the 'tolerance'.

Can we tolerate the tolerance?

The Cp Index

$$C_p = \frac{USL - LSL}{UCL - LCL} = \frac{\text{tolerance}}{6s}$$

- For the process to be inherently capable, the Cp value needs to be at least 1.0
- It may be inherently capable, but how well is it located? You need to use the other capability index, Cpk to find out precisely...

The Cpk Index

For an X moving R chart:

$$C_{pk} = \frac{USL - \bar{X}}{UCL - \bar{X}} \quad \text{or} \quad \frac{\bar{X} - LSL}{\bar{X} - LCL}$$

For an X bar R chart:

$$C_{pk} = \frac{USL - \bar{\bar{X}}}{3s} \quad \text{or} \quad \frac{\bar{\bar{X}} - LSL}{3s}$$

Which one we use all depends on the mean.

So, for an X moving R chart:

So, which one do we use?

- If the mean of the control chart is closer to the customer USL than it is to the LSL, then we use: $C_{pk} = \frac{USL - \bar{X}}{3s}$
- If the mean is closer to the LSL than it is to the USL, then we use: $C_{pk} = \frac{\bar{X} - LSL}{3s}$
- 3s is the difference between the UCL and the process mean

Six Sigma is pretty close to 100%

Process Sigma

Another way of measuring process capability is to use sigma values. They can help baseline process performance against the customer's CTQs, though do remember they tell you nothing about future performance. Sigma values are often expressed as 'defects per million opportunities', (dpmo) as the table below shows. Incidentally, you can see that Six Sigma performance equates to only 3.4 dpmo; almost 100% but not quite!

What would this mean for your organisation?

Yield	σ	DPMO
99.99966%	6	3.4
99.977%	5	230
99.939%	4	6,210
93.32%	3	66,800
69.2%	2	308,000
Right first time percentage	**Process capability**	**Defects per million opportunities**

The table also includes 'yield' figures – the right first time percentage. It's important to recognise that you are looking at 'first pass' performance. In other words, if you made an error but corrected it before it went out to the customer, you would still count the defect. After all, this Non-Value-Added activity would have cost you time and effort. And remember you are looking at defects. Your customer may have several CTQs, and it's possible there may be more than one defect in the transaction.

Key terms

In calculating sigma values for your processes, you need to understand the following key terms:

Defects and Defectives

Key term	Definition
Unit:	the item produced or processed
Defect:	any event that does not meet the specification of a CTQ
Defect Opportunity:	any event that provides a chance of not meeting a customer CTQ. Our approach is that the number of defect opportunities will equal the number of CTQs
Defective:	a unit with one or more defects

You can work out our sigma performance against the CTQs as the following example shows. Here, we have taken a sample of 500 processed 'units'. There are three CTQs, so we have three defect opportunities.
And there are 57 defects.

Putting a value on it…

1. Number of units processed — N = 500

2. Total number of defects made (include defects made and later fixed) — D = 57

3. Number of defect opportunities per unit — O = 3

4. Solve for defects per million opportunities

$$\text{DPMO} = 1{,}000{,}000 \times \frac{D}{N \times O}$$

$$= 1{,}000{,}000 \times \frac{57}{500 \times 3}$$

$$= 38{,}000$$

5. Look up Process Sigma in the Abridged Sigma Conversion Table — Sigma = 3.3

Use the dpmo figure that's closest

Abridged Sigma Conversion Table

Yield	Sigma	Defects per 1,000,000	Defects per 100,000	Defects per 10,000	Defects per 1,000	Defects per 100
99.99966%	6.0	3.4	0.34	0.034	0.0034	0.00034
99.9995%	5.9	5	0.5	0.05	0.005	0.0005
99.9992%	5.8	8	0.8	0.08	0.008	0.0008
99.9990%	5.7	10	1	0.1	0.01	0.001
99.9980%	5.6	20	2	0.2	0.02	0.002
99.9970%	5.5	30	3	0.3	0.03	0.003
99.9960%	5.4	40	4	0.4	0.04	0.004
99.9930%	5.3	70	7	0.7	0.07	0.007
99.9900%	5.2	100	10	1.0	0.1	0.01
99.9850%	5.1	150	15	1.5	0.15	0.015
99.9770%	5.0	230	23	2.3	0.23	0.023
99.9670%	4.9	330	33	3.3	0.33	0.033
99.9520%	4.8	480	48	4.8	0.48	0.048
99.9320%	4.7	680	68	6.8	0.68	0.068
99.9040%	4.6	960	96	9.6	0.96	0.096
99.8650%	4.5	1,350	135	13.5	1.35	0.135
99.8140%	4.4	1,860	186	18.6	1.86	0.186
99.7450%	4.3	2,550	255	25.5	2.55	0.255
99.6540%	4.2	3,460	346	34.6	3.46	0.346
99.5340%	4.1	4,660	466	46.6	4.66	0.466
99.3790%	4.0	6,210	621	62.1	6.21	0.621
99.1810%	3.9	8,190	819	81.9	8.19	0.819
98.930%	3.8	10,700	1,070	107	10.7	1.07
98.610%	3.7	13,900	1,390	139	13.9	1.39
98.220%	3.6	17,800	1,780	178	17.8	1.78
97.730%	3.5	22,700	2,270	227	22.7	2.27
97.130%	3.4	28,700	2,870	287	28.7	2.87
96.410%	3.3	35,900	3,590	359	35.9	3.59
95.540%	3.2	44,600	4,460	446	44.6	4.46
94.520%	3.1	54,800	5,480	548	54.8	5.48
93.320%	3.0	66,800	6,680	668	66.8	6.68
91.920%	2.9	80,800	8,080	808	80.8	8.08
90.320%	2.8	96,800	9,680	968	96.8	9.68
88.50%	2.7	115,000	11,500	1,150	115	11.5
86.50%	2.6	135,000	13,500	1,350	135	13.5
84.20%	2.5	158,000	15,800	1,580	158	15.8
81.60%	2.4	184,000	18,400	1,840	184	18.4
78.80%	2.3	212,000	21,200	2,120	212	21.2
75.80%	2.2	242,000	24,200	2,420	242	24.2
72.60%	2.1	274,000	27,400	2,740	274	27.4
69.20%	2.0	308,000	30,800	3,080	308	30.8
65.60%	1.9	344,000	34,400	3,440	344	34.4
61.80%	1.8	382,000	38,200	3,820	382	38.2
58.00%	1.7	420,000	42,000	4,200	420	42
54.00%	1.6	460,000	46,000	4,600	460	46
50%	1.5	500,000	50,000	5,000	500	50
46%	1.4	540,000	54,000	5,400	540	54
43%	1.3	570,000	57,000	5,700	570	57
39%	1.2	610,000	61,000	6,100	610	61
35%	1.1	650,000	65,000	6,500	650	65
31%	1.0	690,000	69,000	6,900	690	69
28%	0.9	720,000	72,000	7,200	720	72
25%	0.8	750,000	75,000	7,500	750	75
22%	0.7	780,000	78,000	7,800	780	78
19%	0.6	810,000	81,000	8,100	810	81
16%	0.5	840,000	84,000	8,400	840	84
14%	0.4	860,000	86,000	8,600	860	86
12%	0.3	880,000	88,000	8,800	880	88
10%	0.2	900,000	90,000	9,000	900	90
8%	0.1	920,000	92,000	9,200	920	92

Measure – a quick summary

Phew! So that's the Measure phase completed. It can be quite hard work, but you should now know how the work gets done; and how well it gets done. The data can help you baseline performance and determine the gap.

Simply understanding the process flow can help you identify opportunities for improvement. Process Stapling and the development of a Deployment Flow-chart or Value Stream Map are key activities in this respect. But make sure you map what really happens; not what you think happens. The Process Mapping builds on your SIPOC and helps you see the Non-Value-Add steps and the bottlenecks in the process. It also helps you identify where you need to measure.

You may have determined the CTQs already, but if not, you must do so in this phase. The CTQs will aid your understanding of what you are trying to do, and, of course, they form the basis of your measurement set.

Determining the Project Y and the likely Xs will help focus your project and may well lead to a more effective set of ongoing operational measures using Control Charts. SPC is so important in helping you understand variation, highlighting when you need to take action and when you don't. Of course, the data that emerges is only as good as the process that collects it. If you want to manage by fact, you must manage your Data Collection Process.

Confirm the CTQs

Update the SIPOC

Develop Deployment Flow-chart or Value Stream Map

Agree the Output Measures (Ys)

Ideally, agree the Input and In-Process Measures (Xs)

Implement the Data Collection Plan

Display the data on Control Charts

Determine the baseline performance

Update the Improvement Charter, Storyboard and Communications Plan

Step 3 – Identify & check the possible causes

What's this step all about?

In Measure you discovered what's really happening in your process. Now you need to identify why it's happening, and determine the root cause. You need to manage by fact, though, so you must verify and validate your ideas about possible suspects. It's too easy to jump to conclusions.

There are two broad routes to finding the vital Xs – either through the 'process door' or the 'data door'. That said, you'll usually need to do both. Carrying out Analyse properly will help you in determining the solution when you get to the Improve phase.

Clearly, the extent of analysis required will vary depending on the scope and nature of the problem you are tackling, and, indeed, what your 'Measure' activities have identified. Essentially, though, you are analysing the process and the data.

The key outputs

- Identification of the Non-Value-Added steps and any bottlenecks, and an understanding of how well the process flows – your Deployment Flow-chart or Value Stream Map will help you here, especially if you have also captured unit and cycle time data
- Identification of Waste – Process Stapling and a Spaghetti Diagram will help in spotting this, especially wasted movement and transport, as well as any unnecessary activities, and, of course, you may well have collected data on errors in the process
- Identification of the possible causes – probably displayed on a Fishbone Diagram
- Identification of the key drivers (key Xs) – using an Interrelationship Diagram
- If not already in place, agreed input and in-process measures (the Xs)
- Data analysed and displayed properly for easy understanding. This might include Control Charts and Pareto Diagrams, and will help you verify and validate the possible causes
- Validation of the root cause and vital few Xs – probably using a Scatter Diagram
- An updated Improvement Charter
- An updated Storyboard
- An updated Communications Plan
- Where appropriate, an updated Stakeholder Analysis

- Are we confident we have identified the root cause(s)?
- Given the importance of the Benefits Review that follows, are we confident that we are able to Quantify the Opportunity?
- Remembering the elephant, and the need for 'bite-size' chunks, can we address all the root causes identified?
- Do we feel this process can be repaired and improved?
- Who needs to be working on the project now?
- What's needed on communications?
- Have we reviewed the Stakeholder Analysis?

Key questions before moving on

Key tools for this step

Understanding the Process Flow

As we indicated earlier, it's likely that you will need to analyse how the work gets done and how well it gets done. In terms of how the work gets done, you need to properly understand the process flow, identify constraints and bottlenecks, determine the most effective and efficient location of people and their equipment, and assess the pros and cons of adopting a pull rather than push approach.

We have already looked at the Deployment Flow-chart, Value Stream Mapping, Process Stapling and Spaghetti Diagrams. Toyota's Production System and Goldratt's 'Theory of Constraints' are covered on pages 99 and 103 as part of the Improve phase, but they are highly relevant here in Analyse, too, and cover the principles of single piece flow, Cell Manufacturing and the use of a pull system.

Seven Wastes

Your Process Stapling exercise, and the development of the Spaghetti Diagram may well have identified a number of Non-Value-Add steps and wasted movement. And your Data Collection activity will have helped you quantify the level of defects and rework.

Identifying and removing waste is an important element in improving performance.

Hello Muda...

The Japanese refer to waste as Muda. They describe two broad types of Muda and seven categories.

In any process, there will be steps that add value, but also those that do not. Some of these Non-Value-Add steps have to stay, however, perhaps because of limitations in available technology or resource, for example. But other Non-Value-Add steps can be eliminated there and then, perhaps through a DMAIC project. In waste terms, these are described as 'Type one' and 'Type two' Muda respectively. Within these broad types of waste, Toyota's Taiichi Ohno identified seven categories:

- **Overproduction** – producing more than is needed or earlier than is needed by the next process or customer. This type of waste contributes to the other six
- **Waiting** – people unable to process their work due to equipment failure, for example
- **Transportation** – moving materials and output unnecessarily. This might include sending partly completed batches of work through the internal mail system because of the inappropriate location of processing teams. It could also involve moves that go to and fro' or that include Non-Value-Add steps
- **Processing** – performing unnecessary processing steps, involving, for example, irrelevant information, or the completion of too many fields
- **Inventory** – this particularly links to overproduction resulting in too much work in progress, for example, or too much stock of brochures, leaflets or stationery

- **Motion** – too much movement for people, perhaps due to the inappropriate siting of process teams or equipment, or the need to find misplaced documents. This type of waste could also include the need to access too many screens, double handling, or the need for unnecessary approvals
- **Correction** – dealing with rework caused by not meeting customer requirements, providing incomplete replies, or simply making errors

All this waste is expense!

How's your PONC?

American quality guru Phil Crosby refers to PONC – the price of non-conformance. It's a simple measure that puts a price on how much it costs to do things wrong, to not meet the customer requirements (CTQs). He estimates that in a service organisation, PONC is somewhere between 25-40% of the annual expenditure!

Check Sheets and Pareto Diagrams can be very effective in helping you highlight and analyse at least some of these categories of waste.

A simple Check Sheet could capture defect types, or reasons for complaints, for example, with the resulting data presented in a Pareto Chart to help highlight the vital few areas to focus on. In the example below, the Type A defects have been broken down by day of the week to help get to the root cause. You might want to break things down further, perhaps by hour of the day, but you should also look to see if there are lessons to learn from the apparently better performance on Wednesdays.

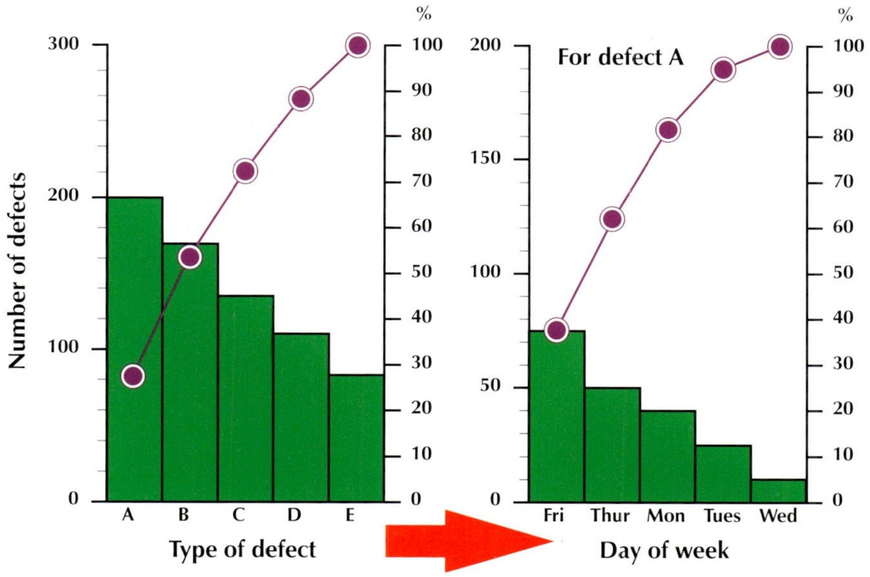

The Pareto Diagram is a simple, but effective way of presenting defect and waste data, but remember the need to weight things. There may be more type A defects, but perhaps they are relatively cheap and easy to put right. Type C defects, on the other hand, are less in number, but may be very expensive. Recasting things by cost, for example, may give you a very different picture.

Pareto analysis of errors

Take care with the weighting…

Pareto Analysis

Pareto was an Italian economist. He observed that 80% of the country's wealth is in the hands of 20% of the population. In an improvement context 20% of the issues or Xs cause 80% of the effect on the Ys. The 80:20 rule won't always be exact, but there's likely to be a 'vital few' Xs causing 'most' of the problem(s). You need to find them. The Pareto Chart presents and ranks data in order, showing those factors which occur most frequently. It's a way of presenting data effectively, particularly when you have segmented results. The 'cumulative percentage' line helps highlight the vital few.

In this example, using the data from the Check Sheet on page 53, you can easily see the two main issues that need to be addressed:

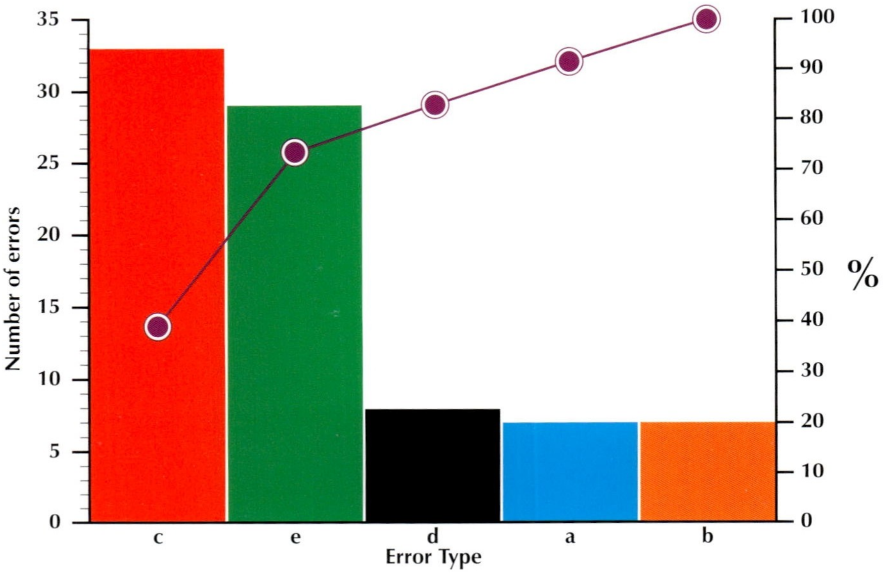

The example was straightforward. It might not be in your improvement project – before taking action, remember to weight the Pareto Analysis, perhaps by cost or risk. It might be that this will present a very different picture.

Brainstorming and Negative Brainstorming

Whether you are looking for possible causes or solutions, Brainstorming is a means of generating ideas; as many as possible in as short a time as possible. It involves all the members of a team. A facilitator helps, but isn't essential, provided some simple rules are followed.

There are a number of different approaches. This workbook will cover some of them; you might evolve your own approach. Either way, there are some sensible ground rules:

- Review the subject to be brainstormed and ensure everyone understands the purpose of the Brainstorming session. What question are we addressing?
- Allow a minute or two of silence to think about the question

- Generate ideas – (see below)
- Capture ideas – (see below)
- Never criticise or at this stage discuss the ideas. The 'silly idea' often spawns a creative approach to an issue
- Review the ideas, and perhaps group and present them as a Fishbone or Affinity Diagram

Generating ideas can be done in any of the following ways...

- 'Structured': in this method, the team members each give an idea in turn, or 'pass' until the next round. When, say, three or four people 'pass' in a row, open it up for general input
- 'Unstructured': here, team members simply put forward their ideas as they come to mind. It's a less formal approach, but there's a danger of someone dominating the session
- 'Silent': this approach helps ensure everyone is involved. The team members write their ideas onto Post-its. One idea per Post-it

The detailed rules for silent brainstorming are covered in the Affinity Diagram.

Apart from the silent brainstorm, capturing ideas is usually actioned by one team member writing the various ideas onto a flipchart. This should capture the speaker's words and not be the interpretation of the recorder. Writing onto Post-its can be sensible as these can be posted up onto a wall or flipchart when everyone has finished writing ideas, and can then be reviewed and grouped in a relatively easy way. This can be an effective way of developing a Fishbone Diagram.

Accentuate the positive by being negative

Sometimes, generating ideas can be made more fun, and more effective, by carrying out a Negative Brainstorm. You might, for example, brainstorm ways to ensure meetings are a disaster, or customers are unhappy. 'Changing the signs' can provide a list of actions to help achieve your real aim, or you can ask the question, "how many of these things are we doing?" The answer might surprise you!

Brainstorming is at the heart of many of the 'creative tools and techniques' covered in the Improve phase, including, for example, CATALYST and the Idea Box.

It's Kipling... no it isn't!

Is/is not

Kipling comes into the frame yet again, in this simple technique that helps you logically analyse a situation and move towards the root cause of something.

You can use the six honest serving men, or at least some of them, to help you see any trends. Does a problem only occur on certain days, for example, or in specific locations, or when the temperature is above a certain point, and so on. Naturally, this technique links to the segmentation and stratification of things.

The technique can also help you develop your Problem Statement in the Improvement Charter, and may be useful in thinking about the scope of the project.

Kipling	Is	Is not
What		
Where		
When		
Who		
How		
Why		

And don't forget that the approach can help you identify solutions, too. Your analysis may help identify best, or at least better practice.

The following table provides a more comprehensive set of questions and prompts to help in your use of this technique:

		Problem Profile		Get more information on
		Is	Is not	
What	Process/Service	What Process/Service has the defect?	What similar Process/Service(s) could have had the defect but have not?	
	Defect	What is the defect?	What other similar defect(s) on the defective Process/Service could have been observed, but were not?	
Where	Seen on Process/Service	Where specifically on the Process/Service do you see the defect?	Where else on the Process/Service could you have observed the defect but did not?	
	Seen geographically	Where geographically, is the defective Process/Service observed?	Where else geographically, could you have observed the defective Process/Service, but did not?	
When	First seen	When was the defect first observed?	When could it have been first observed, but was not?	
	When seen since	When, since the first observation, has the defect been observed?	What other time pattern of occurrence of the defect could you have observed but did not?	
	When seen in process flow	When is the defect seen in the process flow or production and distribution?	When else in the process flow might you have observed the defect, but did not?	
	When seen in operating cycle	When is the defect seen in the operating cycle of the Process/Service?	When else in the operating cycle might you have observed the defect, but did not?	
	When seen in life cycle	When is the defect seen in the life cycle of the Process/Service?	When else in the life cycle might you have observed the defect, but did not?	
How big	How many Process/Services have the defect?	How many Process/Services have the defect?	How many in total and how few Process/Services could have been affected by the defect but were not?	
	How many/much defect(s) per Process/Service?	How much or how many defect(s) per Process/Service?	How much or how many defect(s) per Process/Service could have been observed but were not?	
	What is the trend?	How has the quantity trend developed since first observation and what is it now? (Static/erratic, getting better/worse).	How else could the quantity trends have developed but did not, and what else could it be now, but is not?	

Fishbone Diagram

There's a time and a place for the Fishbone

The Fishbone or 'Cause and Effect' Diagram is a useful way of grouping and presenting ideas from a brainstorm. What are the possible 'causes' of this 'effect'? Using Post-its during the brainstorm will make this easier, rather like the Affinity Diagram, though with a narrower more focused issue statement.

Take care to remember that cause and effect will be separated by time. One doesn't always immediately follow the other; indeed, there could be months, or even years between the two!

Remember too, that conducting a 'negative Fishbone' can be a creative way of doing this. You could then 'highlight' those things you are doing for real.

The causes can be grouped together under whatever headings you choose. Traditional headings are People, Equipment, Method, Materials, and Environment.

The traditional headers can be useful in prompting ideas during the brainstorm, though they can also inhibit more lateral thinking.

Construct the Cause and Effect Diagram by:

1. Placing 'the issue or problem statement' in the head of the fish on the right hand side of the diagram. It can help if this is phrased as a question – e.g. "what are the causes of...?" or "why does this occur?" Keep the questions quite narrow unless you plan to develop a whalebone!
2. Drawing the traditional major cause headings on the left hand side of the diagram, or your own headers as appropriate. These are the main bones.
3. Placing the brainstormed ideas under the appropriate major categories, and
4. For each possible cause, ask: "why does it happen?" and list the responses as branches off the major causes. These are the smaller bones. In doing this, ask "why?" five times; get under the real reason (see page 80).

The resulting diagram should look a bit like a Fishbone! Your next steps will be to look for possible causes that appear repeatedly, and to identify where you need to gather data through measurement. As you measure these various Xs you can update your diagram to show whether your suspects are guilty or not. In determining this you are likely to use a Scatter Diagram.

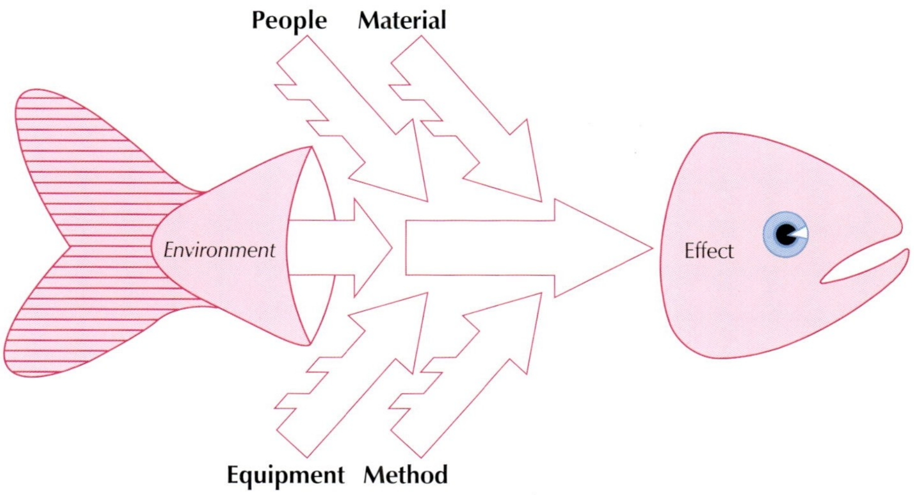

Ask the right questions

Ask Why

But, do remember to ask the right "why?" – the one that helps to get you to the root cause or challenges the previously held assumptions.

All too often, people have forgotten why something is done the way it is. And all too often, the reasons are no longer relevant!

The six honest serving-men, described in these opening lines from a Rudyard Kipling poem, provide an effective framework for a series of open questions.

Mr Kipling does ask exceedingly good questions!

"I keep six honest serving-men
(They taught me all I knew);
Their names are What and Why and When,
And How and Where and Who."

Use them all, but particularly "Why." Ask "Why?" five times, or as often as you need, to get to the real answer, that's beyond the initial, often superficial first response, as this example shows:

Dressing up the five whys?

Why am I always late for work?
Because the bus I have to take goes the long way round

Why? Because I usually miss the more direct bus

Why? Because I leave the house late

Why? Because it takes so long to get ready

Why? Because I can't decide what to wear

So, the problem isn't really the bus service, it's the choosing what to wear. The solution could be as simple as selecting and laying out your clothes the night before.

Finally, in asking questions, it's important to know what you are likely to do with the answers – sometimes finding the answers can be expensive in terms of time and effort. Always try to begin with the end in mind.

Interrelationship Diagram

Understanding the relationships

The purpose of the 'ID' is to identify the logical and sequential connections and relationships between the clusters that were generated in the Fishbone Diagram or in a more complex Affinity Diagram. It can also be used in the same way to look at the ideas within a cluster, for example focusing on the main driver that emerges.

What you are trying to do is to determine whether there is a cause and effect relationship between each and every pair of clusters. And if there is, which cluster is causing the effect.

Typically, it will be on the lines of:

- "Must this happen here before that can happen?"
- "You must do this first in order to achieve that."
- "Does one item tend to help or influence the other?"
- "Does one item tend to follow the other?"

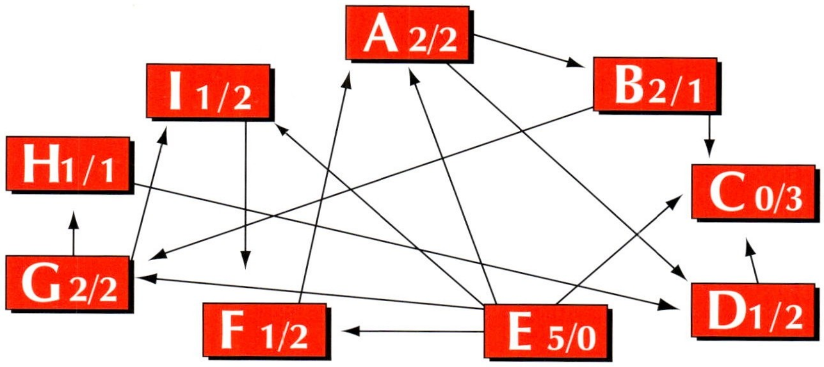

The process is as follows:

Did you get the headers right?

1. Take the header cards from the Affinity or Fishbone Diagram and place them in a circle, perhaps on a flipchart. Remember that these were meant to stand on their own in terms of capturing the sense and content of the various clusters. Let's see if they do!
2. Essentially, it's a question of looking at each pair to determine if there's a relationship. So, if the headers are A, B, C, D and E, you would start with A and look at AB, AC, AD and AE. Then you would move to B and look at BC, BD, BE and so on.
3. Where there is a relationship, you draw a line connecting the two headers.
4. You then need to determine the causal cluster and turn the line into an arrow, by drawing the arrowhead into the header that is being effected.
5. Once all the headers have been reviewed in this way, you count the 'arrows out' and the 'arrows in' for each header. This will enable you to identify the key causal factors.
6. From this, you can determine the likely sequence of actions now needed to get to the root cause and/or progress the project. In the example above, 'E' is clearly the most upstream cluster; as we mentioned earlier, you can increase your focus with a further ID on this main driver.

There are a few simple rules to keep to. They're simple, but you will find it difficult to stick to them.

The rules are simple but...

- You might want them, but 'two-headed arrows' are not allowed.
- Don't use thin lines and thick lines, or dotted lines. There's either a relationship or there isn't.
- That said, it can be sensible to use a pencil until everyone is sure on the lines and the direction of the arrows.
- If you reach an impasse, skip it and come back to it later. By that time it might be easier to resolve.

The ID is hard work, but it really does help increase understanding and provide insights that will help ensure the subsequent success of the project.

We plough the fields & scatter…

Scatter Diagram

A Scatter Diagram helps identify whether there's a relationship between two variables. What's more, you can put a value on the relationship if there is one. We're talking cause and effect, Xs and Ys.

It's used to help verify potential root causes. You are looking to see if a change in the cause values (the Xs) will produce a change in the effect values (the Ys). If your suspected cause is a real one, the Y variable will change as the X variable changes.

The dependent Y variable is always plotted vertically; the independent X variable is plotted on the horizontal axis. **The data is plotted in pairs** – so when X = 'this value,' Y = 'that value'.
The example highlights 4 such pairs:

Is there a relationship?

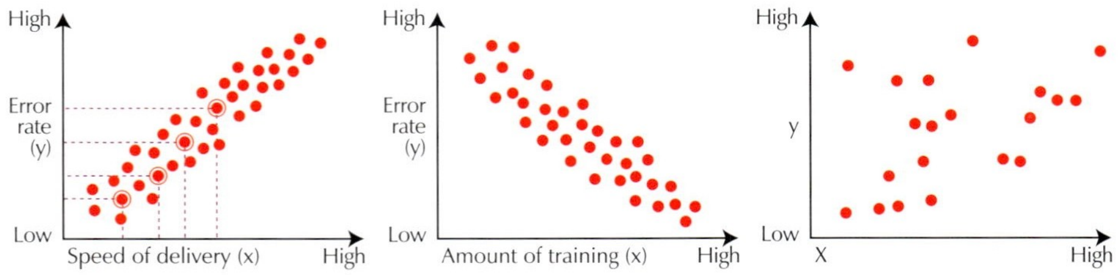

Positive Correlation
In the example, there seems to be a relationship between speed and error rate – the faster we do it, the more errors we get. It's a positive correlation – the values of Y increase as the values of X increase.

Negative Correlation
The second example shows a negative correlation – the values of Y decrease as the values of X increase.

No Correlation
And in the third example, there's no relationship at all.

Scatter Diagrams are easy to produce using spreadsheets like Excel or programs like Minitab. But it's important to be aware of some of the common errors and pitfalls associated with them. These include:

- mixing up the X and Y variables and axes
- data is incorrectly paired
- the diagram is not 'square' because of inappropriate scaling
- the scaling is not sensitive enough for the data

Ideally, the scale should contain 5–15 increments of equal width on each axis, otherwise you may see some odd patterns. If you use Excel, beware of 'autoscaling' that ignores this requirement. If you are collecting data in 'seconds' then plot the data in 'seconds,' not in minutes or hours. Rounding data up or down may mean the scale is not sensitive enough and this can also lead to unusual patterns.

Make sure the correlation is a cause and effect relationship

Finally, the biggest mistake can be the assumption that correlation implies causation. This won't always be true – use common sense to draw your conclusions.

What's under the gooseberry bush?!

The example below shows data from the German village of Oldenberg, for the years 1930 to 1936. It clearly shows that Walt Disney's Dumbo cartoon got it right. Storks really do bring the babies!

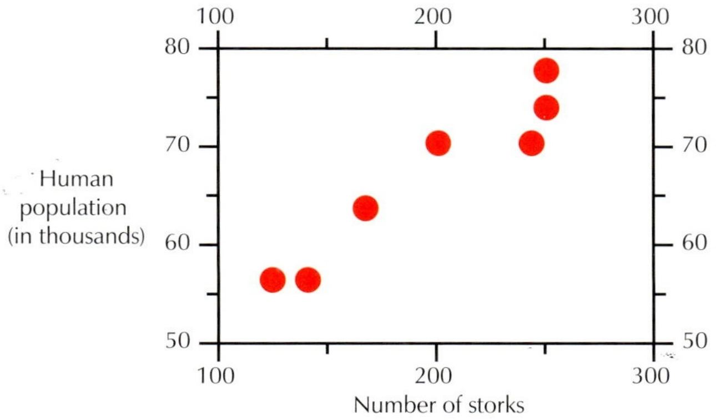

In case you are wondering, the X and Y axes are the wrong way round. The village expanded in this period. The new houses, built for the increasing human population, had tall chimneys that proved to be an attraction for nesting storks.

Have you found the vital few?

The correlation co-efficient is expressed as r.
In a perfect positive correlation, r = +1;
In a perfect negative correlation, r = -1.
Expressed as a percentage, r^2 shows the percent of variation in Y explained by the effect of X. So, if r = 0.7, the variable is causing 49% of the variation in Y; if r = 0.8, the value increases to 64%. In either of these circumstances, it seems you have found the important root cause of the problem.

Your spreadsheet software can give you this value which is a key factor in confirming the vital few root causes.

Drawing the line...

The correlation co-efficient leads on to a high level introduction of Regression and the 'line of best fit'. It is easy to draw a line through highly correlated data such as that in the first two examples on page 82. This enables you to make predictions for the value of Y with different values of X, though remember that the straight line might not continue forever. There may well be a future threshold where things change dramatically.

Going into regression...

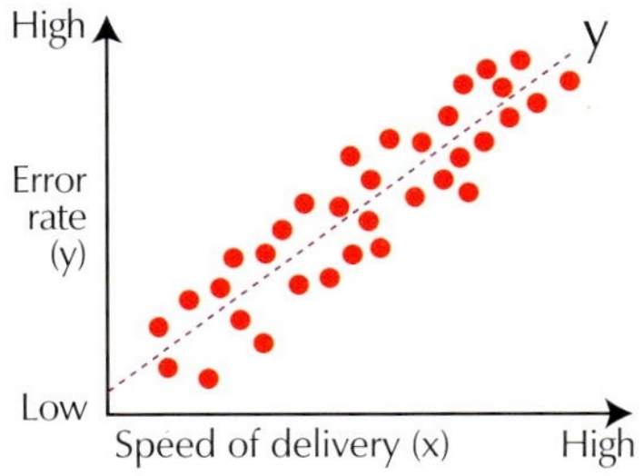

The line can be calculated precisely by using the line, or regression equation,

$y = b_0 + b_1x$ where:

b_0 = the intercept (where the line crosses the vertical axis, x = 0)

b_1 = the slope (the change in y per unit increase in y)

This is known as Linear Regression when there is just one X. Multiple Regression extends the technique to cover several Xs. These are presented as a collection of Scatter Diagrams in a Matrix plot. The equation becomes:

$y = b_0 + b_1x_1 + b_2x_2 + b_3x_3 +$ etc.,
where b_2=slope for x_2 and b_3=slope for x_3

So what's the difference?

Hypothesis Testing

From time to time, and particularly where you have been segmenting your process data, you will need to know whether there is a statistical difference between data sets. The data might show, for example, the results from different teams, perhaps from varying locations. Or you may have been experimenting with improvement ideas and want to know whether the apparent improvement in your results is real.

You might be able to see a difference by viewing the shape of the data in a histogram, for example, or by comparing the mean or standard deviation, or indeed, the amount of variation. But even if you appear to see a difference, how different is different? You know about natural variation, so is the difference you are seeing 'real', or is it simply chance variation?

So, can we infer that the data has come from the same population, or from a different population? It might be that the sample represents the future population to come. How will you know if the data is really different?

Hypothesis testing helps you find out if there is a statistically significant difference or not. This booklet provides an overview of the tests, which are well supported by software programs such as Minitab, and which are usually covered in detail as part of Black Belt training.

What's the alternate?

The first step is to create two hypotheses for your tests, the null hypothesis, and the alternate hypothesis. The null hypothesis, usually expressed as H_O proposes there is no difference in the data. The alternate hypothesis H_A states there is a difference.

When you use Control Charts, you follow some rules that help identify whether the data is in statistical control. The main rules to identify special causes are set out below as a reminder:

- A point outside the control limits
- A run of seven points, either:
    - All above the mean
    - All below the mean
    - All going up
    - All going down

Provided your chart doesn't exhibit any of these rules, you can feel pretty sure that the data is natural variation. The tests look to provide a reasonable basis for decisions. What you are trying to do is to ensure that, as far as possible, you don't treat natural variation as though it were special cause, or special cause, as though it were natural. Control charts are used to help you make this judgment about ongoing data, with the control limits set at the most appropriate and economic level, +/- 3 standard deviations (99.73%).

What do you see?

In effect, this is a form of hypothesis testing. The null hypothesis is that the data is natural variation; the alternate hypothesis is that it is special cause. When you're not using Control Charts, you need some other tests, unless the difference is absolutely clear as with the following example:

How confident are you?

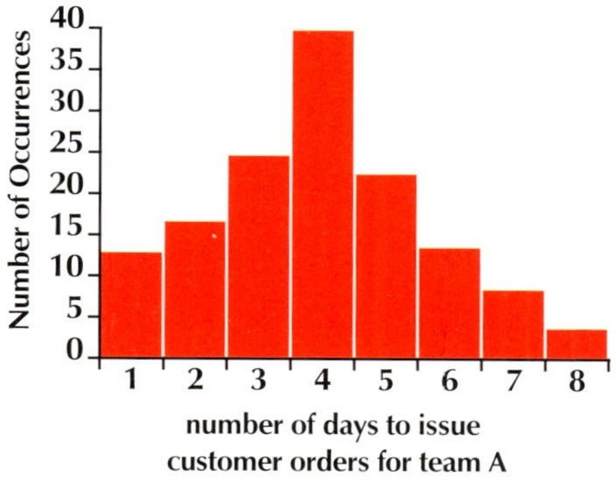

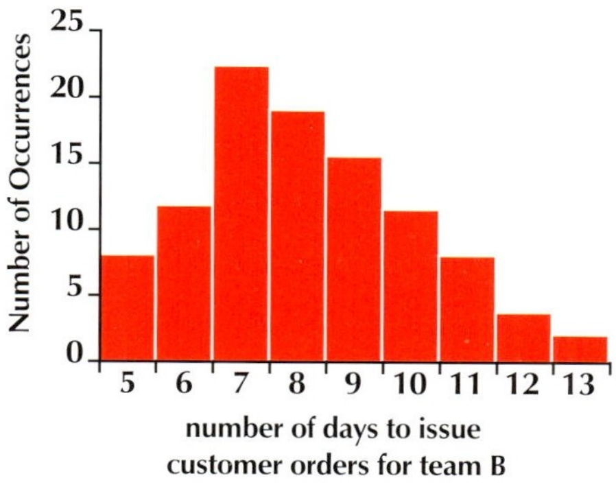

Here the difference is clear, but it's not always so easy to tell.

The hypothesis tests we are looking at are different from Control Charts. They don't look at ongoing data, but rather take a sample at a point in time. And the usual confidence level used is 95% (two standard deviations).

Testing testing testing…

More often than not, you will use one or other of the following three tests:

- T-test (looking at two sets of data)
- ANOVA (looking at three or more sets of data)
- Chi-square (for observed frequencies of two discrete variables)

It depends on whether you are looking at two sets of data or more, and whether the X variables involved are discrete or continuous. The table below provides the basis for selection of the appropriate test.

		Y: Continuous Data	Y: Discrete Data
X	**Continuous Data**	Regression*	Logistic Regression*
X	**Discrete Data**	ANOVA / t–test / Paired t–test†	Chi–Square test

* The regression topics are introduced with the Scatter Diagram & covered in detail as part of Black Belt training

† The paired t–test is where comparison is being made against a standard

Some typical examples of these tests include:

- Determining whether a process change has really improved performance (T-test). So, you are looking at the before and after results
- Identifying 'best' practice groups (ANOVA)
- Test marketing of products to see if the percentage of people opening a new account depends on the marketing method and/or their lifestyle, for example (Chi-square test)

Back to p values...

You use p values to determine whether there is a real difference. Given the usual confidence level of 95%, if p is less than 5% (p = <0.05), we can be 95% confident there is a difference. There is still a 5% chance of spuriously seeing a difference when one isn't there, but the odds are overwhelmingly (19 to 1) against this being the case.

If p is equal to or greater than 5% (p> or = 0.05), then you can conclude there is insufficient evidence to reject the null hypothesis. You can interpret this as either:

- The samples come from the same original population, or
- You have too much variation, or
- Your samples are too small to detect any real difference

Why is it different?

Where there is a difference, in the performance of teams at different branches, for example, don't jump to conclusions about why. The difference could be to do with the way the data is collected, the size of the branch, the number of staff, their experience, the market segmentation, and so on. You need to find the reasons, so you can build in best practice or find ways to eliminate the root causes of problems.

Hypothesis tests are used in Regression and Design of Experiments to confirm that individual Xs are indeed correlated with the Ys (and that overall the regression is significant).

Design of Experiments (DOE)

I was working in the lab late last night...

This technique is used both in the Analyse and Improve phase of projects. The principle, at least, is very straightforward, and software programs such as Minitab take away the complexities of the calculations involved, though interpretation, and, indeed, the implementation of experiments, may need some expert support.

In a way, 'design' is a misnomer, as the technique is really about designing and running experiments to find out whether, and to what extent, the X variables are interacting to influence your process Ys. It may be that you sense there are such interactions, or that historical data is inconclusive or unreliable, in which event, DOE provides a way forward.

We've all done this before...

Almost certainly we have all conducted experiments, even if we didn't know it! Think about travelling to work. You may well have tried different methods of travel, including for example, car, bus, or train, or you may simply have walked, or taken your bike. It's also likely you will have tried different routes, too, perhaps according to when you are travelling. It might be quicker to take one particular route during school term-time, and another when the children are on holidays, for example.

So what are the factors?

Still with travel in mind, think about the different 'factors' influencing the fuel consumption we achieve from our cars. These variables include speed, tyre pressure, and the use of air conditioning among others. But how do you find the most efficient combination of these variables, taking into account the different 'levels' that might be used? The answer is to run a series of experiments trying out the various combinations of factors and levels.

Often, the levels are viewed rather like attributes, so, for example, something is present or not present, or high or low, and so forth. They can also be continuous, though this will make for a much more involved design, with resulting complexities in the interpretation.

Are you on the level?

So, keeping our fuel consumption example simple, lets have two levels in our DOE. High or low speed, say 60 mph or 40 mph; high or low tyre pressures, perhaps 35 psi or 25 psi, and the air conditioning will either be on or off.

X1	X2	X3	Y
Speed (mph)	Tyre pressure (psi)	Air conditioning (on/off)	Miles per gallon?
Low	Low	Off	?
High	Low	Off	?
Low	High	Off	?
High	High	Off	?
Low	Low	On	?
High	Low	On	?
Low	High	On	?
High	High	On	?

The table identifies the eight experiments needed to find the best combination. As you can see, the factors or variables have been labelled X1, X2, and X3, with the output, our fuel consumption, labelled as Y. It's all about cause and effect, independent and dependent variables.

The formula to find the number of experiments needed is the number of levels to the power of the number of factors. So, in this case two levels to the power of three factors.

$2^3 = 2 \times 2 \times 2 = 8$.

What's the form?

Let's look at another example, this time from an office environment. As many as 15% of customer order forms are incomplete, and cannot be processed as a result. The improvement team brainstorm some ideas to remedy the problem, including:

- Providing a reference to a summary of the key requirements on the internet web-site
- Highlighting the key fields on the order form
- Providing a leaflet with information and examples of a correctly completed form

Rubik meets DOE

These become the three factors, so again, we have eight experiments to conduct, since there are two levels, in this case, present or not present. In Minitab, the results are presented as a 3D cube. Some people find these easy to read; others don't. The picture is built up like this:

The improvement team reduces the incomplete forms to 11% by providing a summary of the key requirements on the internet web site (so the summary on the web is either 'present' or 'not present'). As the 3-D cube builds up, you will see that the results on the left hand side are without the summary, while those on the right are with a summary.

The results at the top of the cube are where highlighted fields have been used; at the bottom they haven't been. So, introducing the highlighted fields and the web summary reduces the problem to 5%. The highlighted fields on their own reduce the problem to 6%.

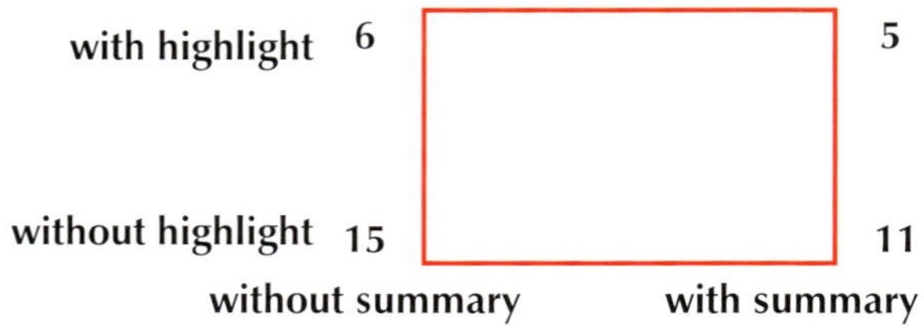

Here's the complete cube. The results at the back are where the leaflet has been included; at the front, the leaflet has not been sent. Providing the leaflet produces the best result when combined with the highlighted fields. Surprisingly, perhaps, there is a 12% error rate when the key summary on the web is also included. It's possible the customer is confused or frustrated with too many things to look at.

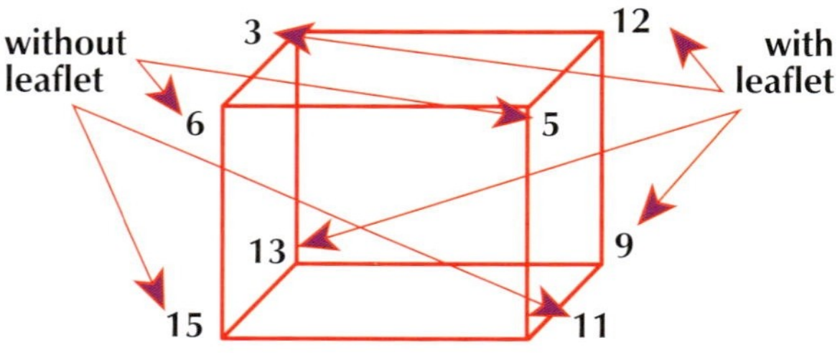

- On the left side of the cube, the results are where there is no key summary on the web; on the right side, there is
- At the top of the cube these results are where highlighted fields have been included; at the bottom the fields have not been highlighted
- At the back of the cube all these include the leaflet with the information and examples; at the front they don't
- And where they meet at the corners you have the results for the various combinations

As you can see, the best combination is…? If you are still not sure, please refer to the table on the next page.

DOE can be a very helpful tool in analysing data in order to find the vital few causes of a problem, or to test out improvement ideas. But there are some real issues to bear in mind. Do you use historic data or new? If the data exists, can you be sure of its accuracy? And if you need to collect new data, how many experiments can you realistically run?

X1	X2	X3	Y
No Summary	No Highlight	No Leaflet	15
Key Summary	No Highlight	No Leaflet	11
No Summary	Highlighted	No Leaflet	6
Key Summary	Highlighted	No Leaflet	5
No Summary	No Highlight	Leaflet	13
Key Summary	No Highlight	Leaflet	9
No Summary	Highlighted	Leaflet	3
Key Summary	Highlighted	Leaflet	12

Only you will know the answer, but remember that with only 5 factors and 2 levels you're up to 32 experiments. And with only 3 more variables involved, the number is up to 256! What's more, you may feel it sensible to replicate the experiments in order to feel more comfortable with the results. The trick lies in the selection of which particular experiments to undertake. Without careful assessment, the technique can become impractical.

Can you do that many?

One way of reducing the logistics and costs is to conduct a 'partial' rather than 'full factorial', so for example running 8 experiments instead of 16. Minitab will give you the numbers and combinations to run, but recognise that by averaging some of the data, which is effectively what the software does for you, there is some risk that the results miss something in the higher order interactions.

Inevitably, your approach will be a compromise that takes account of the time and cost involved, and, not least, your own patience! The important thing to remember is that a good design can produce excellent results, including some occasional surprises.

DOE tends to be used most often in manufacturing, where its applications can be highly complex, and where the need for specialist support is likely. But it has its uses in service and transactional processes, particularly in the analysis of historical data. And, as the example has perhaps shown, these can be relatively straightforward.

If nothing else, DOE might encourage you to find ways to improve your fuel consumption and reduce costs!

DOE fuels improvement

Analyse – a quick summary

So, that's the Analyse phase. If you have done it properly, you will have identified the root cause of the problem you are tackling. Sometimes this can be straightforward, but often there are surprises when you manage by fact and avoid jumping to conclusions. The usual suspects may not be guilty after all. That said, sometimes, the root cause will be very easy to spot, perhaps as a result of Process Stapling, where Non-Value-Add steps are clear to see, for example.

Tools and techniques like the Fishbone and Interrelationship Diagrams can prove very helpful in understanding the drivers behind the problem you are tackling. Though it might not always be so, you are likely to need some data to confirm things and to provide the evidence. And you may well find a need to segment that data to help get to the real root cause.

Either way, using a Scatter Diagram and determining the correlation co-efficient values can be an effective way in proving your analysis is correct.

Your Tollgate Review is especially important here, since before moving on to the Improve phase, you need to Quantify the Opportunity, assessing all the Non-Value-Adds and determining, for example, whether to continue with the project or re-scope it in some way.

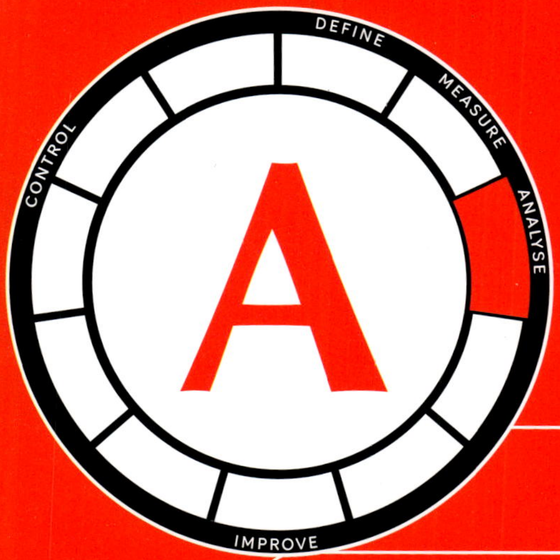

- *Identify the NVA steps and waste*
- *Identify the bottlenecks and constraints*
- *Generate ideas about the possible causes*
- *Use a Fishbone Diagram to group the possible Xs*
- *Identify the key driver(s)*
- *Use data to validate the suspects*
- *Confirm the root cause*
- *Update the Improvement Charter, Storyboard and Communications Plan*

Review – Quantify the opportunity

What's this step all about?

In addition to the Tollgate Reviews, there are three Benefit Reviews in the Lean Six Sigma Improvement Journey. Apart from looking at benefits, they provide an opportunity to step back, assess progress, and ask some general questions on the following lines:

- How are things going?
- Are we on course?
- What have we learnt?
- What's gone well, and why?
- What conclusions can be drawn?

The primary focus of this first Benefit Review, however, is to Quantify the Opportunity – to really understand the extent of Non-Value-Add activities and waste, and the potential for improvement. When you completed Step 2, you were able to understand the current situation and level of performance. Having completed Step 3, your level of understanding should have increased significantly:

- You will know why performance is at the level it is
- You should understand the costs involved in the process, both overall and at the steps level
- You will have identified the waste and the NVA steps, including the rework loops, and understood their impact on your ability to meet the CTQs

In Quantifying the Opportunity you first need to calculate the saving if all this waste and NVA work were eliminated, making sure you document your assumptions. You may feel the opportunity is too small to bother about, or so large it justifies widening the scope of the project, or developing a phased approach using a Multi-Generation Plan.

Either way, this is the time to review and agree your project goals, sensibly estimating what is possible for your project.

The key outputs

- An agreed estimate that Quantifies the Opportunity
- The documented assumptions behind the assessment
- An agreed project goal
- An updated Improvement Charter, Communication Plan, & Storyboard
- Where appropriate, an updated Stakeholder Analysis

Key questions before moving on

- Are we comfortable with the assumptions behind our Quantified Opportunity figures?
- Do the agreed goals for this project make sense?
- If we have decided to break the project into phases, do these different 'generations' link together sensibly?
- Given the project goals, do we need to review our team membership?
- Have we updated our Improvement Charter, Storyboard, and Communications Plan?

Key tools for this step

Takt Time

There are several 'Lean measures' that can help you understand performance and the scale of improvement needed. These could have been included within the sections on Measure or Analyse, but we have included Takt Time here, and Overall Process Effectiveness, in the Control section on pages 129 and 130.

Takt Time tells you how quickly you need to action things, given the customer demand

And the beat goes on

Takt is German for a precise interval of time such as a musical meter. It serves as the rhythm or beat of the process – the frequency at which a product or service must be completed in order to meet customer needs.

The Takt Time formula is the available production time divided by the customer demand. The available time is independent of how many resources are available. It represents the number of working hours in the day or shift.

For example, if a widget factory operates 480 minutes per day and customers demand 240 widgets per day, Takt Time is two minutes. Similarly, if customers want two new products per month, Takt Time is two weeks. It's important to recognise the effect of rework – if you have a 10% error rate, for example, your Takt Time is effectively reduced in direct proportion.

Be tactful with takt

Calculating Takt Time

Let's take an example, using our formula:

$$\frac{\text{The available work time per shift}}{\text{The number of customer orders per shift}}$$

- **We have 100 customer requests each working day, where we have an eight hour shift for 10 people**
- **The number of people isn't a factor in calculating Takt time, so:**
  - **8 (hours) x 60 (minutes) = 480 available minutes**
  - **480 divided by 100 (customer requests) = 4.80 Takt time**
- **Even if there were 20 people, the Takt time would still be 4.80**
- **It's the production rate needed to meet the demand**

Incidentally, Toyota typically reviews the Takt Time for a process every month, with a tweaking review every 10 days. Within a service organisation, the use of Control Charts to understand the likely variation in customer orders, for example, can be a helpful way of reviewing Takt Time.

So, if you are looking to provide 'same day' service or delivery, for example, this measure will help you understand the size of the task ahead. In turn, this might help you identify the need to use a Multi-Generation Plan to break the project into bite-sized chunks.

Multi-Generation Plan

It's a generation thing…

Often, you know where you want to be, but recognise that getting there will take some time and effort. It's likely to be achieved in a series of projects rather than in one hit.

The MGP provides the basis for a series of projects for your products, services, and processes, perhaps over several years. It is based around the concept of a 'step – stretch – leap' strategy.

Each 'generation' looks to focus on a different aspect of meeting market and customer requirements, with the longer-term aim of securing market leadership. The typical three-part strategy is on the lines of:

An opportunity to learn…

In the first generation of a product or service, and, in the management and improvement of the supporting processes, you are looking to take remedial action and close the gaps in order to prevent the defection of customers to competitors, for example. This might include identifying and closing gaps in the market itself.

The second generation looks to build on this by enhancing your processes further, and perhaps developing products and services that target new markets, or the customers of our competitors, or win back the customers you lost.

Finally, in the third generation, you try to achieve market leadership through breakthroughs. These might be in technical expertise, productivity, or exceptional service, or perhaps, through some combination of all of these.

Developing a MGP helps present a vision of what you are trying to achieve, but does so in a way that highlights the phases and rationale behind the approach. And, of course, you can incorporate the feedback and learning from one generation into the future generations of the product or process.

This should help you manage risks and contain costs more effectively, and lead to a smoother and perhaps faster transition to the longer term desired state. It's a technique that also fits very well in Step 1, though you'll still need to review things at the end of Step 3 as your understanding of the project is more detailed and you can 'Quantify the Opportunity'.

Step 4 – Generate possible solutions

What's this step all about?

The Improve phase is where most people will have wanted to start! Now you have identified the root cause of the problem, you can begin to generate improvement ideas to help solve it. Your ideas will need to be reviewed and prioritised, and perhaps even tested on a small scale before, selecting the most appropriate in Step 5. In Step 6, the chosen solution may need to be developed in more detail, but will almost certainly need to be properly piloted.

Sometimes, the improvement solution is very straightforward; or at least it might seem to be. Your Process Stapling and Value-Add Analysis may have identified several steps that can be removed from the process, for example, or a Spaghetti Diagram may have highlighted the need to re-site people or equipment to reduce wasted travel and movement. The reduction of batch sizes or a move to a pull not push process flow may be the answer.

Some opportunities for prevention, for example FMEA or Jidoka, may also provide readily identifiable solutions, but it's likely you will need to use Brainstorming in its various guises to help you. Negative Brainstorming can be especially helpful. The Fishbone Diagram that we introduced in Step 3 could also be used to group your improvement ideas. Here, the question in the head of the fish would be on the lines of 'how can we reduce cycle time in the order process?', or 'how can we reduce errors in order processing?', for example.

Where practical, it's sensible to run a small-scale pilot or test to check things out. This can help ensure there are no unexpected knock-on problems down-stream, and can also make the selection process easier in Step 5.

The key outputs

- Where appropriate, a number of potential solutions that genuinely address the problem
- Where appropriate, a 'future state' Deployment Flow-chart or Value Stream Map
- Where appropriate, the results from any tests or pilots you have run
- A 'sense of confidence' that you are ready to select the most appropriate solution!
- An updated Improvement Charter, Communication Plan, and Storyboard

Key questions before moving on

- What are the possible solutions?
- How did we generate these ideas?
- Which possible solutions seem to best address the root cause(s) identified in Step 3?
- What are the advantages and disadvantages of these?

Key tools for this step

Lean Thinking Tools and Techniques

As we indicated in the introduction to this step, sometimes the improvement solution is clear. Often this can be the result of using techniques like Process Stapling and the Spaghetti Diagram which may have highlighted the need to re-site people or equipment to reduce wasted travel and movement.

Your Process Stapling may also have identified the need to apply some 5Ss activity to tidy the work place up, or will have helped you spot some ergonomic related issues that are slowing things down.

Time for a tidy up?

Five Ss

The Five Ss provide a simple housekeeping checklist to help reduce waste and wasted effort in the work place. In a way, there is a link to the concepts of Just in Time, in that the aim is to have the tools and materials you need to do the job, when you need them.

From six serving men to Five Ss

Implementing the Five Ss should lead to a safer and more pleasant working environment, and one that encourages both self-management and team working. The Five Ss are set out below:

- **Sort** encourages you to look at the tools, materials, equipment and information you need to do your job, and separate them into those used 'frequently', 'occasionally', and 'never'.

  This might be done based on your experience, but 'tagging' the items in some way can be helpful. You could, for example, tag the various items on a particular date, then see when next you use them. If you haven't used them in, say, one month, then move to Straighten.

Do you really need to keep that?

- **Straighten** is literally about straightening things up. Putting everything you use frequently easily to hand. This might include, for example, toolkits, files, or e-mail folders, or could involve moving a printer or copier to a convenient location.

  Things that you don't use frequently need to be put somewhere else or thrown way! You will need to decide how many items need storing, how they should be stored and where. Naturally, these should be appropriately labelled to facilitate their easy access in the future.

The right things in the right place...

- **Scrub** is about keeping the things you use, and the environment you work in, clean and tidy, and appropriately maintained. You want the work place to shine.

  So, get rid of rubbish and dirt, and don't leave scrap lying around. Make sure your tools are current, safe, and clean, and that all the information and documents you use are up to date and well presented. And make sure that equipment and machinery are routinely serviced and maintained as they should be.

Keep it clean!

- **Systemise** is about strengthening your approach. Design a simple way of working so that your tools and information stay sorted, straightened and scrubbed. Essentially, this means regularly re-doing the first three Ss!

Make it a way of life...

...and for life

This should help identify the reasons why the work place becomes messy and cluttered, and prompt preventive thinking to find ways of stopping the problems recurring

- **Standardise** the whole approach. In other words, keep doing it. Stick to this system every day, train everyone in the application of the Five Ss, regularly review things, and tell others about your effective method of working

Ergonomics

Some years ago, researchers compared the relative positions of the controls on a lathe with the size of an average male worker. It was found that the lathe operator would have to stoop and move from side to side to operate the lathe controls. An 'ideal' sized person to fit the lathe would be just 4.5 feet tall, 2 feet across the shoulders and have an arm span of 8 feet!

People come in all shapes and sizes

This example epitomises the shortcoming in design when no account has been taken of the user. People come in all shapes and sizes, and ergonomics takes this variability into account in the design process.

Ergonomics is about ensuring a good fit between people, the things they do, the objects they use, and the environments in which they work, travel and play. There are a range of best practice guidelines available covering things like lifting and the ideal design of workstations, for example.

We're all different

One goal of ergonomics is to design jobs to fit people. Job design in ergonomics recognises everyone is different! Variability in height, weight, length of arms, size of hands and so on, needs to be taken into account, and study of the human body (anthropometrics), gives data on how these things vary across the population.

There is a very logical process to go through in applying these principles:

- First analyse the job – what is required to do the job properly and safely?
- Identify any stressful elements of the job, focusing on issues related to physical movement. So, is machine access too tight for the largest worker, do short workers have to crane their necks to read displays, do workers have to reach above shoulders or below their knees, for example?
- Determine the relevant body dimensions linked to the problems identified. Is it height, size, arm length, or hand size for example?
- Decide how much variability needs to be accommodated in the design
- With the help of the operators and users, redesign the workstation as appropriate, building in adjustment capability to accommodate size or arm length differences between staff

Benefits are improved efficiency, quality, and job satisfaction. The costs of failure include error rates and physical fatigue, or worse.

An introduction to the Toyota Production System

Your analysis of how the work gets done may have highlighted Non-Value-Add steps and bottlenecks, and your data will have helped you quantify things. It may also have highlighted peaks and troughs in the volume of items being processed, for example.

Lean Thinking focuses on reducing waste and improving process flow. Toyota's Production System 'house' provides an effective framework, and introduces a number of the key Lean concepts and tools:

The house in front...

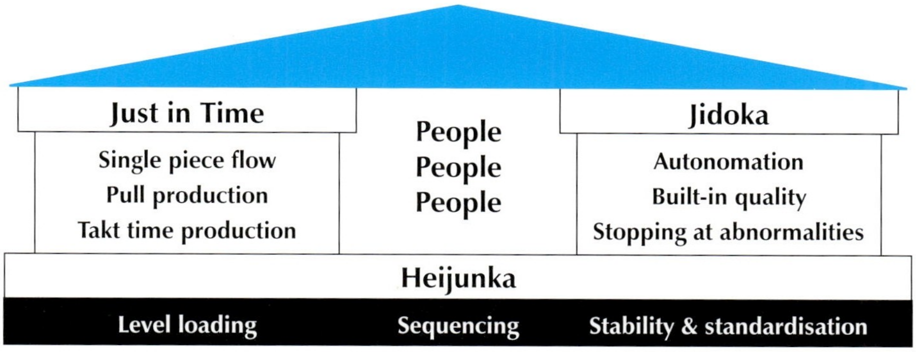

As with our own approach, people are at the heart of the Toyota Production System.

Their approach to the 'softer issues' includes focusing on developing exceptional people and teams who follow their company's philosophy. They do this by:

- Creating a strong and stable culture where values and beliefs are widely shared and lived out over many years
- Training exceptional individuals and teams to work within the corporate philosophy to gain exceptional results
- Constantly working to reinforce the culture
- Using cross-functional teams to solve problems
- Teaching individuals how to work together as teams

Don't waste potential...

Importantly, we all need to involve the people in the process, equipping them to be able, and feel able, to challenge and improve their processes and the way they work. Indeed, an eighth category of waste is not utilising the creative potential of people.

But, what are the other elements of the Toyota House, especially those using the Japanese terms?

Are you on the level?

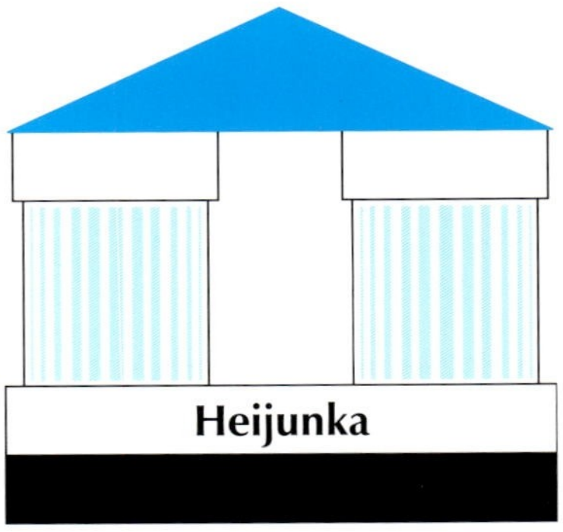

Heijunka provides the foundation; it encompasses the idea of smoothing the processing and production by considering levelling and sequencing. For a process to run smoothly and consistently with many different kinds of output, it has to average, not just in volume, but also in kinds.

Levelling involves smoothing the volume of production in order to reduce variation. Amongst other things, this seeks to prevent 'end-of-period' peaks, where production is initially slow, but then quickens in the last days of the sales or accounting period, for example.

Sequencing involves mixing the kinds of work processed. So, for example, when setting up new loans, the type of loan being processed is mixed to better match customer demand, and help ensure applications are actioned in date order.

Buffer the vampire slayer?!

It may be easier to manage this in manufacturing where a producer may be able to place a small buffer of finished goods near shipping, to respond to the ups and downs in weekly orders. Keeping a small stock of finished goods at the very end of the value stream, this producer can level demand to its plant, and to its suppliers, making for more efficient utilisation of assets along the entire value stream while meeting customer requirements.

It's Standard!

The third strand of Heijunka seeks to reduce variation in the way the work is carried out, highlighting the importance of following a standard process and procedure. This links well to the concept of Process Management and the Control Plan, where the process owner continuously seeks to find and consistently deploy best practice.

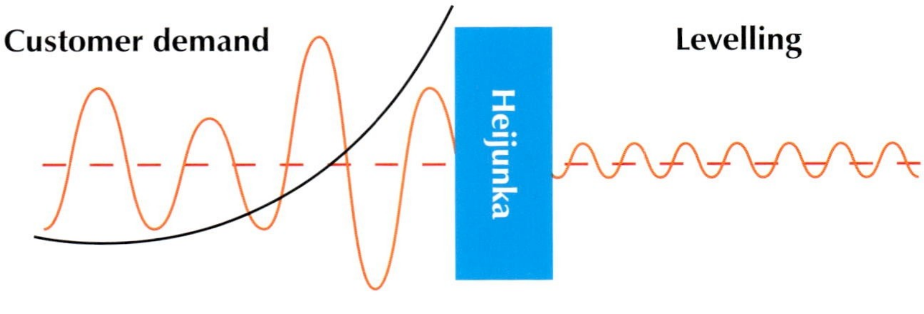

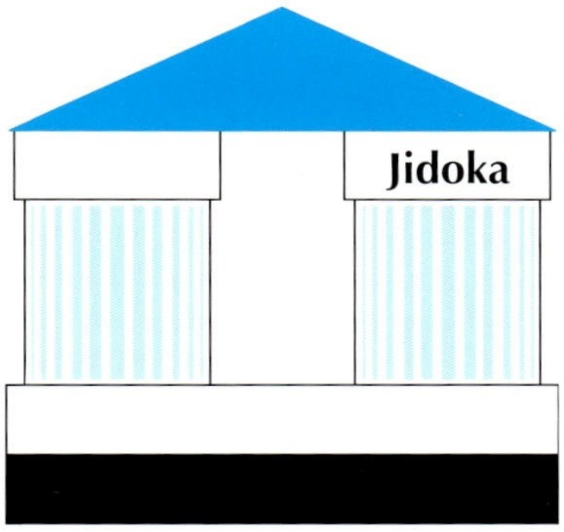

Jidoka is about prevention; it links closely with Error Proofing and FMEA. There are two main elements of Jidoka; both seek to prevent work continuing when something goes wrong:

Autonomation allows machines to operate autonomously, by shutting down if something goes wrong. It's a concept also known as automation with human intelligence. The 'no' is underlined to highlight the fact that no defects are allowed to pass to a follow-on process.

In 1902, Sakichi Toyoda, the founder of the Toyota group, invented an automated loom that stopped anytime a thread broke. A simple example today would be for a printer to stop processing copy when the ink runs out.

Prevention is looming. A stitch in time saves nine…

Without this concept, automation has the potential to allow a large number of defects to be created very quickly, especially if processing is in batches; autonomation is a means of preventing defective items from passing to the next process.

Stop at Every Abnormality is a concept where a manual process stops whenever an abnormal condition occurs. In manufacturing, you may have heard of the concept where every employee is empowered to 'stop the line', perhaps following the identification of a special cause on a Control Chart. Forcing everything to stop and immediately focus on a problem can seem painful at first, but is an effective way to quickly get at the root cause of issues. Again, this can be especially important if you are processing in batches.

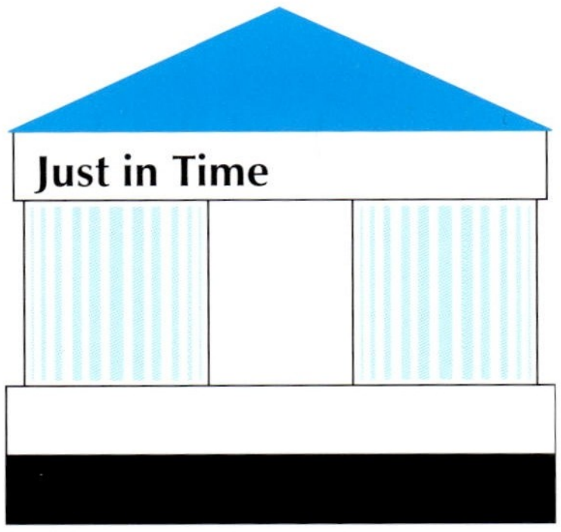

Just in Time provides the customer what is needed, when it's needed, and in the quantity it's needed. The concept applies to both internal and external customers:

Are you just in time?

Single Piece Flow means each person performs an operation and makes a quick quality check before moving their output to the next person in the following process. If a defect is detected, Jidoka is enacted; the process is stopped, and immediate action is taken to correct the situation and take countermeasures to prevent reoccurrence.

Ideally, this single piece continuous flow processing is carried out within 'cells'. This involves locating the relevant people and machinery more closely together (see page 103).

Beware the batch

Either way, it's a real change of thinking that moves us away from processing in batches. Traditionally, large batches of individual cases are processed at each step and are passed along the process only after an entire batch has been completed. The delays are increased when the batches travel around the organisation, both in terms of the transport time, and the time they sit waiting in the internal mail system – at any given time, most of the cases in a batch are sitting idle, waiting to be processed. In manufacturing, this is seen as costly excess inventory.

What's more, errors can neither be picked up, nor addressed quickly – if they occur, they often occur in volume. And, of course, this delays identifying the root cause. With single piece flow, we can get to the root cause analysis faster, and this helps prevent a common error recurring throughout the process.

The old pull and push?

Pull Production is a system where each process takes what it needs from the preceding process, when it needs it, and in the exact amount needed. In other words, the customer pulls the supply and helps avoid being swamped by items that aren't needed at a particular time. Apart from anything else, this will reduce the need for potentially costly storage space. All too often, overproduction in one process, perhaps to meet local efficiency targets, results in problems downstream. This increases work in progress, and creates bottlenecks. The symptoms include:

- Too many – making more than needed
- Too soon – making them earlier than needed
- Too fast – making them faster than needed

Can you Kanban?

Ideally, the downstream activities signal their needs to the upstream activities through a 'kanban' card or an electronic andon board, for example. And nothing is produced upstream until the signal is flagged. Of course, if the activity is being processed within a 'cell', the operation of 'pull' becomes more straightforward to see and manage.

Cellular Manufacturing and Product Families

Operating a Kanban system is made easier when the people involved in the process are operating in the same work area – where this isn't the case, your Spaghetti Diagram may have highlighted wasted travel time.

Cellular Manufacturing organises the entire process for similar products into a group of team members, includes all the necessary equipment and is known as a Cell. The cells are arranged to easily facilitate all operations, often adopting a horse-shoe shape as the diagram shows:

Cells are often set up in U-shapes

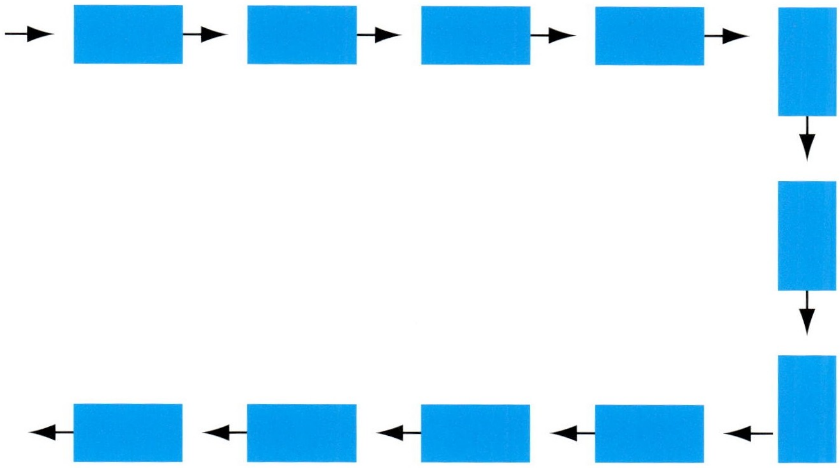

Outputs or parts are handed off from operation to operation eliminating setups and unnecessary costs and delays between operations.

In this type of arrangement, it makes sense for the process cell to identify and process common 'product families'. These are the products or services that have identical or similar processing steps, but which might previously have been seen as different activities each processed by different teams.

Keep it in the family…

Theory of Constraints

Goldratt's 'Theory of Constraints' proposes a five-step approach to help improve flow:

1. Identify the constraint
2. Exploit the constraint
3. Subordinate the other steps to the constraint
4. Elevate the constraint
5. Go back to Step 1 and do it all again

A constraint can be identified where we have a build-up of people (a queue), material (inventory), units to be processed, or work in progress (a backlog).

So, having found the bottleneck or 'constraint', find ways to improve the processing capability at this point in the process flow, as best you can. Use the constraint to dictate the pace at which the upstream activities operate, but search for ways to 'elevate' the constraint. In other words, introduce improvements that remove this particular bottleneck, possibly through a DMAIC project.

Of course, once you've done that, there will be a new constraint somewhere else in the flow, so start this improvement cycle again.

The Deployment Flow-chart highlights bottlenecks. In the example on page 42, 'Brian' is the constraint. We need to see how throughput can be maximised here; we have to exploit the constraint. But while this step is the constraint, it sets the pace for the process. There's no point in 'Ann' pushing output through to 'Brian'; it's a classic application for pull not push.

Of course, once we find a way to elevate the constraint, we need to identify the new bottleneck. In this example, it would be 'Clare'.

It's Buffy again!

Incidentally, there's usually a good case to place a small buffer in front of the constraint to ensure sufficient work is always there, should an upstream process step experience problems, perhaps through temporary machine failure, for example. Given that this upstream step can work faster than the constraint, things should soon catch up, but in the meantime the process flow is uninterrupted. This concept is known as drum, buffer, rope. The drum refers to the beat of production set by the constraint, the rope pulls the work through at the right pace.

Dig that beat, Man!

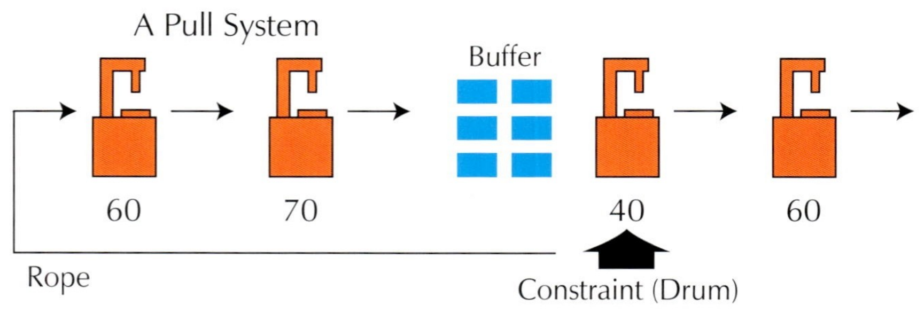

Drum-Buffer-Rope for control

Drum: the pace setting resource – the constraint

Buffer: the amount of protection in front of the resource

Rope: the scheduled staggered release of material to be in line with the Drum's schedule

SMED (Single Minute Exchange of Die)

This concept is one of the real keys to the success of the Japanese motor industry. They worked on reducing the time it took to change over and set up production equipment from one part number to another.

'The Machine That Changed the World' by Womack, Jones and Roos, provides an interesting insight into the background and the events.

SMED refers to the target of doing this in a minute, or at least less than ten minutes! This revolution in thinking enabled them to provide a variety of options to customers without a correspondingly high increase in production costs, something western car producers could not do at the time.

Shigeo Shingo's key insights about set up reduction, which were developed in the 1950s and 60s, were separating the internal set up operations – which can only be done when a machine is stopped, so, for example, inserting a new die – from the external operations that can be performed while the machine is still running, such as transporting the new die to the machine.

These concepts and the challenge to reduce set up time have real relevance in a service environment. You need to think about the time it takes to move from one system or screen to another, for example, perhaps as you deal with different products, services, or enquiry types.

Creative Tools and Techniques

Where the improvement solution is less clear, you may need to generate some creative ideas to solve the problem.

Sometimes, the use of Random Words, pictures or analogies can help stimulate new ideas and ways of looking at problems. There are a cluster of techniques to help you generate these creative ideas – many of them are used with Brainstorming. As you've seen already, Negative Brainstorming can be quite an innovative approach in itself. And using the green hat from Thinking Hats can help you focus on the creative thinking needed in this step.

Have you got a minute?

A catalyst for change

CATALYST

We'll begin by generating ideas with CATALYST using the letters of catalyst to provide a checklist of questions and prompts. This can stimulate creative thinking – an approach that builds on ideas by Alex Osborn.

So, using CATALYST as an acronym, let's generate some ideas:

- **C**ombine – can you combine or merge things in some way, including, for example, process steps, product features or service offerings? Sometimes, you can find real improvements in cycle time, for example, simply by reallocating the activities in a process and merging two or more steps together
- **A**dapt – how can you change the way this process or product is used? Can you make some changes to it that enable you to combine some activities or take on some new features?
- **T**echnology – do changes in technology prompt opportunities for change in what is done or how you do it? Importantly, with the speed of technological change, things you couldn't do, even only a few months ago, might now be possible. Are they?
- **A**nalogy – using analogies can be very helpful in getting people to think differently. By conjuring up an image or feeling, you can open up new ideas and view things from a different paradigm
- **L**isten and learn – what can you learn from your customers, suppliers and staff, or from benchmarking? Can you use some of the things that have been said as a trigger for ideas?
- **Y**in yang – here you need to be looking at opposites; male:female; top:bottom; left:right, and so on. What if you do the opposite? You have already seen the power of Negative Brainstorming – of turning the negatives into positives. Yin yang prompts some other angles to consider
- **S**ubstitute – can you substitute anything? Equipment? Materials? Parts? Components? Features? Steps?
- **T**ranspose or transform – could you reverse or rearrange things, including, for example, the sequence of steps in a process, or the shape of a product? And would this make it easier to produce the output?

Random Words

Can you relate to the idea of random creativity?

There are other options that can be used in a similar way, including Random Words and related words. Random Words can be generated in a variety of ways, including from books and newspapers, by randomly choosing page, line, and word numbers, for example. You might be surprised by the ideas this can stimulate.

Get the picture?

There are other ways of encouraging creative thinking, of course. Instead of using words, why not use pictures or images to stimulate thoughts and ideas? And why not try this in conjunction with something like the Idea Box?

Warming up with some ice breakers

Creativity is a wide subject and in this book, we are touching the surface only. Each and every one of us can be creative, but it's essential to recognise the importance of creating the right environment and culture to encourage this behaviour. It's also important to recognise the need to get people in the right frame of mind. Despite the expression, carrying out some ice-breaker exercises is a good way of warming people up.

Idea Box

Out of the box ideas

The Idea Box combines Brainstorming with a Matrix to help you identify a whole range of possibilities for the design of products or processes.
It's particularly effective with products. The example below gives you an idea of how it works in coming up with the design for a laundry hamper:

Improve design for laundry hamper

	Material	Shape	Finish	Position
1	Wicker	Square	Natural	Sits on floor
2	Plastic	Cylindrical	Painted	On ceiling
3	Paper	Rectangle	Clear	On wall
4	Metal	Hexagonal	Luminous	Chute to basement
5	Net material	Cube	Neon	On door

As you can see, the Idea Box provides lots of possible permutations and the one we've highlighted could be appropriate for a youngster's bedroom, perhaps!

In using the Idea Box, you would create your own column headings and brainstorm ideas under each. If you were writing a short story, the headings might be 'characters', 'obstacles' or 'events', 'aims and ambitions', and 'endings'. For processes, an example might include 'information', 'medium', 'communication', and 'person'.

You can have as many columns and rows as you need. And they don't need to be of equal length, as is the case in the neat and tidy example. What's more, you can use more than one item in each column as you search for the ideal permutation.

This is likely to be the case, where you use the technique to develop service or product feature packages, for example.

Kaizen Rapid Improvement Events

Get on the fast track

Sometimes, improvement can be actioned through a Kaizen Rapid Improvement Event. Using a selection of Lean tools, these typically focus on a specific and narrowly scoped problem. They follow a well defined timetable, usually over six weeks, and can be seen as fast-track DMAIC projects. Teamwork and a real knowledge of the work being done are keys to success.

The approach enables the people in the process to apply their knowledge and ideas to make a 'change for the better' – the meaning of Kaizen.

Step 5 – Select the solution

What's this step all about?

If you have identified and perhaps tested out a number of solutions, you now need to evaluate the options and choose the most effective. In doing so, you will need to take account of your criteria, including any known restrictions on resources. The chosen solution may need to be developed in more detail, but will almost certainly need to be properly piloted as part of Step 6.

A full cost benefit analysis might be possible at this stage but may need to wait until the pilot is carried out as part of Step 6. That said, you should be able to have at least a high level picture of cost benefit, though do ensure the assumptions used have been documented.

There are a number of selection techniques that can be used, both here in Step 5, and more generally, in choosing projects or suppliers, as part of your ITT process, for example. You will also find that tools and techniques like the XY Grid and the Force Field Diagram can also be helpful, especially since you are likely to need to carry out a Stakeholder Analysis again shortly.

The key outputs

- Evidence of a systematic selection process using a Priority Based Matrix, for example
- Documented rationale that the chosen solution will address the root cause
- At least an outline cost benefit analysis
- The documented assumptions behind the assessment
- An updated Improvement Charter, Communication Plan, and Storyboard
- Where appropriate, an updated Stakeholder Analysis – not everyone may like your chosen solution!

Key questions before moving on

- Which of the possible solutions is the most effective in meeting our selection criteria?
- And is it viable in terms of likely cost benefit?
- Which tools were used in making the selection?
- And how did we choose and weight the selection criteria?
- The solution may appear to be the best option, but is it good enough?
- Can it be improved?

Key tools for this step

Paired Comparisons and N/3

Paired Comparisons provide a way to determine priorities and select an improvement action to take, or problem to tackle. They can also be used to prioritise CTQs with customers, or to weight the importance of criteria, perhaps as part of a Priority Based Matrix.

It's a technique that forces you into making choices by looking at each pair from a list of options. These may well have resulted from a brainstorm with your team.

It's a simple technique, but how does it compare?

So instead of asking the participants to identify their top choice, you are asking them to select their preference from each pair, perhaps using the following questions:

- "Which item is the greater cause of customer dissatisfaction or non-conformance cost?"
- "Which action or idea do you feel will solve the problem and/or improve the position?"

So, do you prefer A or B? A or C? A or D? A or E? Having looked at A, move to B or C? B or D? B or E? And so on. You could do this openly, by going round the table, or by issuing a 'voting grid' on the following lines:

Item	Description				
A		A/B	A/C	A/D	A/E
B			B/C	B/D	B/E
C				C/D	C/E
D					D/E
E					

Participants should circle their choices in each of the comparisons. The combined results will then point to the agreed priorities for action.

As a technique, it's easy, but should be supported with data and take account of agreed criteria.

Prune things down with N/3

If you are trying to select from a large list of brainstormed ideas, you might want to prune the list down before using Paired Comparisons. **N/3** is a simple way of doing this.

N is the number of items in your list. So divide this by 3 and give that number of votes to each member of your team to select their top choices – one vote per idea. You can then use Paired Comparisons on the reduced list.

Priority Based Matrix

You have already seen how the Matrix can be used to help display your various measures, and, of course, it can be used in a host of other ways, for example, to provide a skills Matrix – a visual display of the people in your team and their ability to perform the tasks in your area.

As a Priority or Criteria Based Matrix it can be used to help you make selections on things, including solutions, and, indeed, the projects to tackle.

The steps for this are as follows:

- List the ideas or options
- Identify the important criteria in the decision
- Weight these on a scale, perhaps using paired comparisons to help you
- Look at how each option impacts the factors and score out of ten
- Multiply the score by the weighting
- Add up the weighted scores and group into high, medium or low
- Reject the low scoring options
- Evaluate the rest and decide

Weights and measures

Options \ Criteria / Weights	A 1	B 3	C 5	Score (weighted)	Rank	%
Idea one	6 / 6	5 / 15	7 / 35	56	3	62
Idea two	3 / 3	7 / 21	6 / 30	54	4	60
Idea three	1 / 1	8 / 24	8 / 40	65	1	72
Idea four	8 / 8	6 / 18	5 / 25	51	5	57
Idea five	7 / 7	7 / 21	6 / 30	58	2	64

Even where you have identified a clear 'winner,' it is worth making sure that it is an effective option and not simply the best of a bad bunch. The percentage column on the right hand side of the diagram will help you keep a check and balance on things, and perhaps encourage you to look for ways of improving the 'preferred choice'.

Is it good enough?

In the example, idea three provides a 72% solution – will that be good enough? Could you 'borrow' some ideas from the other options to enhance things?

Where the approach is used in a tendering exercise to select a supplier, you would almost certainly use the scores to draw up a shortlist of candidates. The top three suppliers, for example, would then be invited in to make their presentation and pitch.

In addition to helping you select the solution for your project, or the supplier for a particular product or service, the technique might well be used to help you select which projects to tackle in the first place.

Here, the project selection criteria should be based on the organisation's strategic goals and business plans. Choosing the right projects is clearly essential if your Lean Six Sigma initiative is to be successful.
The Management Team would weight each criterion by its relative contribution and importance in achieving its plans, with potential projects then evaluated and prioritised for action.

The Priority Based Matrix provides a useful format for the selection of all sorts of things both within the workplace and outside. At home, for example, you might use it to select the next car you want to buy, or the school you would like your children to attend.

Wherever you use it, one of the important aspects in ensuring the selection process works effectively, is to make sure you have included the right criteria in the Matrix, and have correctly assessed their relative importance.

In the example, we have used a simple rating scale of 1 – 5 (not important – very important). Please remember that you can have several criteria with the same weighting, and might well group them into broad categories of 'high', 'medium', and 'low'.

In terms of how well your various selection options meet the criteria, an alternative to scoring out of 10, is to use percentages in line with the following guidelines:

- 100% Complete satisfaction – objectives fully met
- 90% Extensive satisfaction – all important objectives met
- 75% Considerable satisfaction – majority of objectives met
- 50% Moderate satisfaction – half of the objectives met
- 25% Minor satisfaction – less than half of the objectives met
- 10% Minimal satisfaction – small number of objectives met
- 0% No satisfaction – objectives not satisfied at all

Step 6 – Plan and test the solution

What's this step all about?

You need to make sure that both your solution and the Implementation Plan are going to be effective and that as far as possible, teething problems are avoided. A Pilot is almost certainly needed, and this may also provide the opportunity to build some prevention into your solution.

'Prevention' might be your solution, of course, and there's nothing new in this concept, as you can see:

Before it move, hold it,
Before it go wrong, mould it,
Drain off water in winter before it freeze,
Before weeds grow, sow them to the breeze.
You can deal with what has not happened,
Can foresee
Harmful events and not allow them to be.

LAOTZU (CIRCA 600 BC)

With the Pilot complete, you will be able to present a cost benefit analysis as part of the next Benefits Review in order to justify the implementation. This looks to confirm the effectiveness of your Implementation Plan and the deliverables and business case from the project. In developing your Implementation Plan, you might need to use the Affinity and Interrelationship Diagrams to help prepare for success, and the Tree and Arrow Diagrams to agree the tasks and schedule. A well conceived plan can help avoid misunderstandings or mistakes.

The key outputs

- Where appropriate, a more comprehensive Pilot that helps confirm the suitability of the proposed solution and tests your Implementation Plan
- An agreed Implementation Plan that takes account of the pilot results
- Evidence that the Implementation Plan has been error-proofed
- Evidence that prevention has been built into the solution itself, or that opportunities have been identified, should their implementation fall outside the scope of the project
- An updated Improvement Charter, Communication Plan, and Storyboard
- Where appropriate, an updated Stakeholder Analysis – keep your eye on the soft stuff and the E = Q x A formula!

Key questions before moving on

- How do the Pilot results compare to what was expected?
- The solution may appear to be the best option, but is it good enough? Can it be improved?
- Are we sure we have the right team membership – do we need to involve anyone else in the implementation, and in the Control phase?
- What's the Implementation Plan? And who needs to approve it?
- Have we given sufficient thought to the Handover?
- Has everyone who needs to know about the changes been informed?
- How will the plan be communicated?
- How will the results be measured?
- Given the importance of the Benefits Review that follows, are we confident that we are able to confirm the cost benefit analysis?

Key tools for this step

Piloting

Without a pilot you could be taking a flier

Even if you tested your solution in Step 4, a more thorough Pilot is likely to be helpful. Apart from trying things out in relative safety, pilots also provide a selling opportunity for your approach.

In carrying out a Pilot, do remember to avoid the all too commonly seen pitfalls that include creating an unreal test. All too often, people are so wedded to their improvement solution that the Pilot is made to work. This can be achieved by carrying the test out in a clean and quiet environment, for example, when in reality, it should be conducted somewhere dirty and noisy. Another way to ensure a successful Pilot is to conduct the test with your very best people, as opposed to a cross section of your team with varying skills and capabilities.

Either way, there will almost certainly be scale up issues to face, and without appropriate testing, you may be going live in the mistaken belief that the Pilot went smoothly.

As far as possible, treat the Pilot as though it is a full implementation, and develop an appropriate Implementation Plan. The Tree, Matrix and Arrow Diagrams can help you with this plan which should form the basis of your full scale implementation in Step 7.

Tree Diagram

Developing the actions…

The Tree Diagram provides a framework to break things down into more detail. In the example below, it is helping to develop the output from an Affinity Diagram into actionable items that can be assigned to someone.

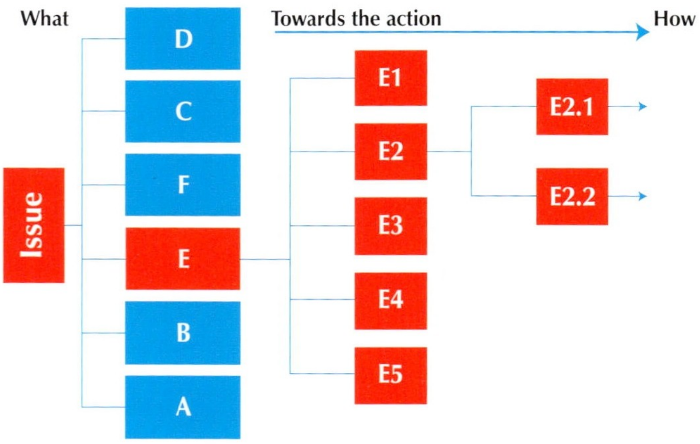

The diagram shows the issue statement from an Affinity Diagram, for example. The second column shows the headers from the Affinity, and the third column sets out the various Post-it notes from cluster E. You will need to look at all of the clusters, of course, but you are starting with E, because it was identified as the key driver in the Interrelationship Diagram on page 81.

So what?

You will be able to move from the 'what' on the left towards the 'how' on the right, by asking questions such as:

- "So what does this mean?"
- "So what actions can be taken to achieve?"
- "So what must we do in order to?"

It might be impossible to action everything on the tree – some items may be mutually exclusive for example. So, look at the major branches and determine whether it's really necessary to include (all) the actions.

In developing the Tree Diagram, remember this is not sequential – so do not worry about sequencing things. What's important is that the last item in each row should be actionable by someone. You will find it helps if you try to line up the last row items and link these to a Matrix to show roles and responsibilities.

Back to the customer again

The Tree Diagram also provides a helpful framework to increase your understanding of customer CTQs. A CTQ tree might look like this:

First level	Second level	
Friendly staff	Willing to answer question	*You will probably need to go down to more levels. And remember the CTQs need to be measurable*
	Shows respect	
Knowledgeable staff	Knows the loan process	
	Knows the market	
	Understands my situation	
Speed	Money when I need it	
	Application fast to fill out	
Accurate	Don't make mistakes	
	Give me the right rate	

A CTQ Tree – 'breaking down' the customer wants and needs to ensure understanding

As you can see, the first level items could be the headers from an Affinity Diagram; the second level could be the Post-its within the cluster. You will need to break things down further – a CTQ tree will often have three levels.

Matrix Diagram

You have already seen how the Matrix can be used to present your various measures. And as a Priority Based, or Criteria Based Matrix, it provides an ideal framework to help in the selection of projects, solutions, or suppliers, for example.

So who is doing what?

Used alongside the Tree Diagram, it can summarise and present who is taking responsibility for the various tasks that have been identified, and perhaps, who needs to be kept informed.

Project tasks from tree diagram	Ann	Brian	Clare	Phil	Jo
	Improvement Team Members				
Design Questionnaire	▲	● (blue)	▲	● (orange)	▲
Issue Questionnaire	● (blue)	● (orange)	▲	▲	▲
Analyse Questionnaire	● (orange)	▲	● (blue)	▲	▲
Present Results	▲	▲	● (orange)	▲	● (blue)

● (blue) Primary responsibility ● (orange) Secondary responsibility ▲ Keep informed

RACI – keeping tabs on who and what

It really helps to make sure that everyone is clear about who is doing what. The Improvement Charter will help pull things together for you in looking at the roles and responsibilities for your improvement team.

RACI provides a simple format for thinking things through not only for your project, but also for day to day to day activities. It's a variation on the Responsibility Matrix, and you need to consider:

- Responsibility
- Accountability
- Consult
- Inform

RACI or ARCI, who CAIRs?!

You might want to present the table as ARCI!

- Who is accountable and for what?
- Who is responsible and for what?
- Who do you need to consult with and on what?
- Who do you need to keep informed and on what?

Either way, you can produce a summary on the following lines that, of course, needs to be updated as part of the ongoing project or operational documentation:

RACI	Who	What
Accountable		
Responsible		
Consulted		
Informed		

Naturally, this information will be of ongoing help in looking at your Stakeholder Analysis and in developing your Communication Plans.

Helping you hit your target

Arrow Diagram

The purpose of this diagram is to establish the time sequence and in doing so, the critical path. It may well be that your project management software will produce this for you, but the Arrow Diagram is a simple way of doing it if not.

And, as you can see on the next page there are similarities with Flow-charts.

Process:

1. Agree the list of tasks and actions needed to complete the plan.
2. Write each task on a 'job or task card'.

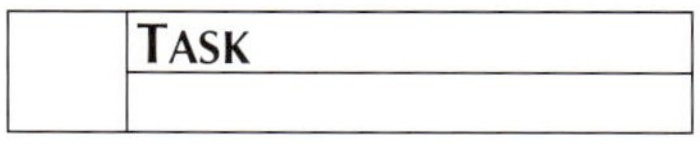

3. Arrange the cards in sequential and parallel order.
4. Check this looks right:
   - 'Which tasks must be completed before we can do this one?'
   - 'Which tasks can be completed while we do this one?'
   - It may be necessary to remove duplicate cards or add new ones as you discover holes.

5. Now you are happy about the sequence of the cards, each one can be allocated a number or letter, as shown.

   Draw solid lines with arrows from each job card to the one immediately following it (A to B to C and so on).

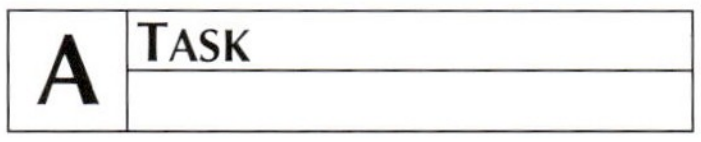

6. Estimate how long it will take to complete each task and record the time on the bottom of the card.

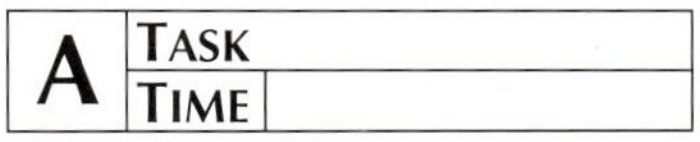

7. Determine the critical path by finding which path has the longest completion time from start to end. This tells you how long it will take to complete this project.
8. Beginning at the start, identify the Earliest Start Time, (EST), each task could be started, given its predecessors and write that number on the card.

9. Beginning at the end and working back, determine the Latest Start Time (LST), each task could be started and still finish the project on schedule.

   Where EST = LST, you have the critical path.
   And where EST and LST differ, you have slack time for that task.

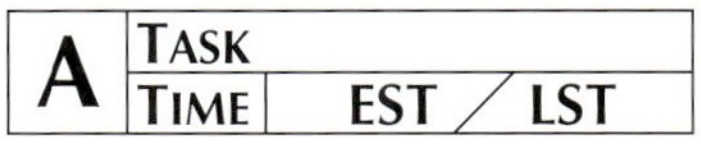

10. Schedule dates for your 'final' plan.

Arrow Diagram – example for delivering course

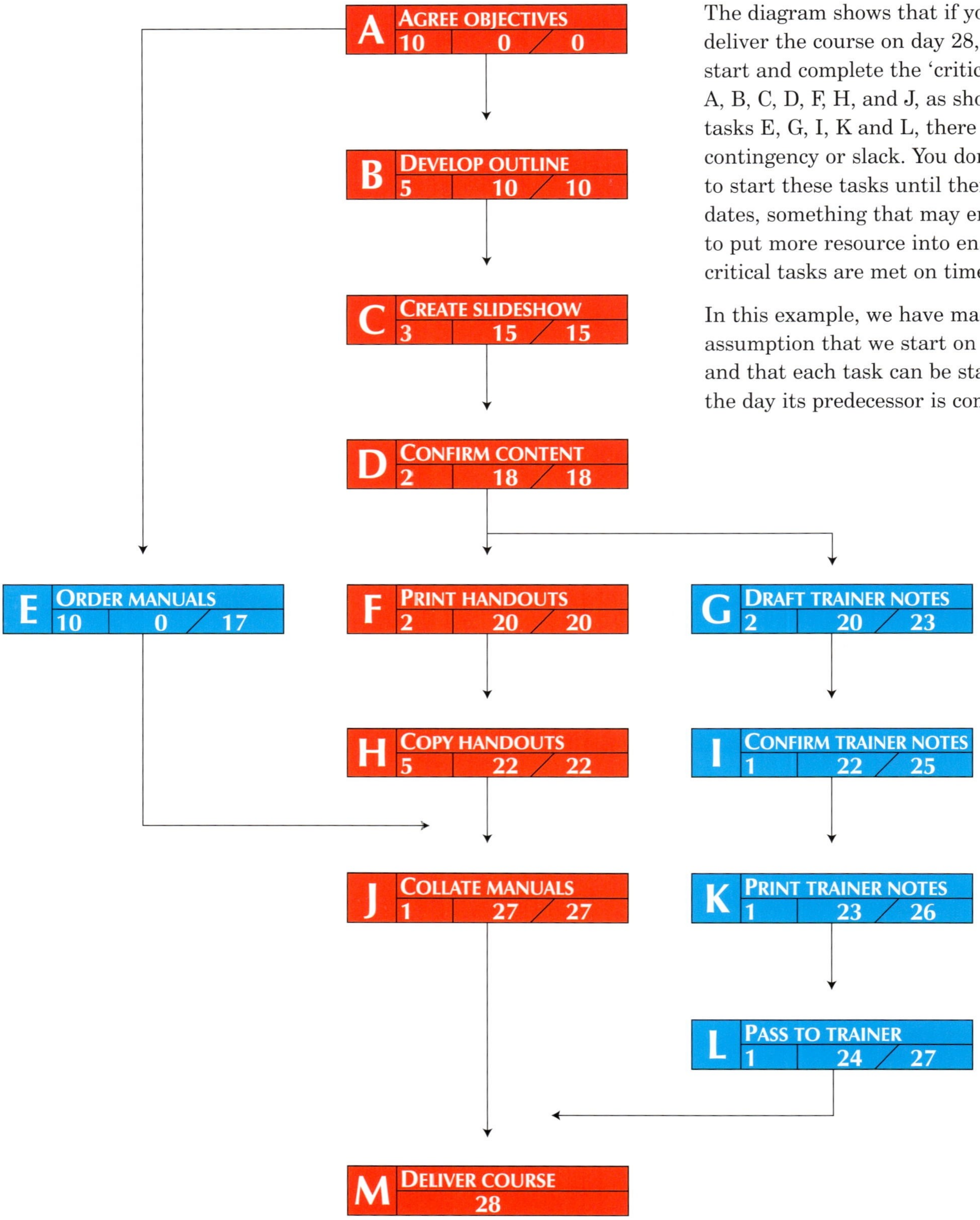

The diagram shows that if you are to deliver the course on day 28, you must start and complete the 'critical tasks' A, B, C, D, F, H, and J, as shown. With tasks E, G, I, K and L, there is some contingency or slack. You don't have to start these tasks until their LST dates, something that may enable you to put more resource into ensuring the critical tasks are met on time.

In this example, we have made the assumption that we start on day zero, and that each task can be started on the day its predecessor is completed.

FMEA and PDPC – tools for prevention

So what might go wrong?

Earlier, we looked at Jidoka; **F**ailure **M**odes and **E**ffects **A**nalysis and **P**rocess **D**ecision **P**rogramme **C**hart are two more of the tools associated with prevention.

The **PDPC** is very easy to use. We covered it in Step 1 as we looked at the risks to a project. You need to use it again to look at the risks to your Implementation Planning.

Essentially, the PDPC looks to identify what might go wrong, how could you prevent it, and what would you do if it still goes wrong?

FMEA is a little more involved. In looking at what might go wrong, you are also trying to assess the impact, how often is it likely to occur, and how likely you are to detect the failure before its effect is realised.

For each of these, you assign a value, usually on a scale of 1 to 10 to reflect the risk. The table on the next page provides a typical rating scale for a service organisation.

The RPN can be used to prompt new projects

To determine priorities for action you need to calculate a 'RPN' – a risk priority number. This value is simply the result of multiplying your ratings for the severity of the risk, the frequency of occurrence and the likelihood of detection. And of course, you need to find ways to reduce the RPN.

Let's go back in time a little and see how they could have applied to a pharmacist. There are lots of things that could go wrong, but as an example, a child could open a bottle of its parents' tablets, take them, and become very ill or die.

Clearly, the severity rating would be high. And so, too, would the detection ratings. The occurrence rating would probably be somewhere in the middle. This 'failure mode' could happen everyday in theory, but either way the pharmacist would be unaware until the damage had been done.

With a high RPN, this failure mode needed to be addressed and so now the pharmacist uses child-proof bottle tops and prints warnings on the bottle about keeping the tablets out of the reach of children. Other actions were taken, too, including making sure that the tablets didn't look or taste like sweets.

Failure Modes & Effects Analysis template

Process: .... **Team:** .... **FMEA Date** (original): .... (revised): ....

What?				Why? When? Where?					How?	Who?	Action Results				
Item/Process Step	Potential Failure Mode	Potential effect(s) of Failure	Severity	Potential cause(s) of Failure	Occurrence	Current Controls and Measures	Detection	RPN	Recommended Actions	Responsibility & Completion Target Date	Action taken	Severity	Occurrence	Detection	RPN

Playing it by the numbers

Rating	Severity of effect	Likelihood of occurrence	Current detectability
1	None	Remote	Immediately detected
2	Very minor effect	Very low	Found easily
3	Minor	Low	Usually found
4	Low to moderate	Low to moderate	Probably found
5	Moderate	Moderate	May be found
6	Moderate to high	Moderate to high	Less than 50% chance of detection
7	High	High	Unlikely to be detected
8	Very high	Very high	Very unlikely to be detected
9	Hazardous	Extremely high	Extremely unlikely to be detected
10	Disastrous	Almost certain	Almost impossible to detect

How could we ensure it goes wrong?!

In coming up with your RPN, do remember that these numbers are subjective and use common sense in determining the action needed.

Ideally, you need to consider each step in your (new) process and identify the failure modes. You can generate your ideas through discussion or Brainstorming. Negative Brainstorming is a particularly good way of doing this – how can we ensure 'this' goes wrong?

Error Proofing

Whether you are designing new processes or improving existing ones, error proofing is a key activity. It may well be the solution itself.

It is sometimes referred to as Poka Yoke – the Japanese slang for "avoiding inadvertent errors." Shigeo Shingo is credited with much work to formalise the approach. His book 'Zero Quality Control: Source Inspection and the Poka Yoke System' is regarded as the classic work on the subject.

So what is it? Essentially, it's the use of process or design features to prevent errors or their negative impact. An error proofing device is often simple and inexpensive, but nevertheless prevents defects from being made.

According to Shingo there are three types of error proofing device: 'contact', 'fixed value', and 'motion step', and with each of these you need to look at the options for control and warning.

Square pegs in round holes

The Contact Type is based around products having a physical shape that inhibits mistakes. This makes it impossible to install parts in any but the correct position. The design of today's electronic equipment, and its various attachments and extensions, for example, ensures the right cables can only go into the right sockets. This is achieved through a combination of part sizes and shapes, as well as colour codes. Another example would be a fixed diameter hole through which all products must fall. Any oversized product will be prevented from passing through, and therefore the potential defect associated with it is prevented.

The Fixed Value method helps make it clear when a part is missing or not used, but essentially ensures appropriate quantities. A simple example would be the French fry scoop used in a 'burger bar'. A further example is 'egg trays' used for the supply of parts – if any compartment in the egg tray is empty then it is easy to spot that something is missing.

The 'Motion Step' automatically ensures that the process operator has taken the correct path or number of steps, possibly breaking a photocell light sensor, or stepping on a pressure sensitive pad during the assembly cycle. A very different example is how spell-checkers provide automatic warnings when words are incorrectly spelt throughout the completion of a word processing document.

Implementation Plan/Handover

If you have treated the pilot as though it were a full implementation, then developing the final Implementation Plan for real should be a relatively straightforward task.

To ensure success, however, you will need to ensure an effective handover. It's so easy to make assumptions about who is responsible for what, and for things to fall down between the cracks. Ideally, the handover should be treated as a contract between the relevant parties, but either way, the Matrix Diagram and the adoption of RACI should help avoid any misunderstandings.

Improve – a quick summary

As you will have seen, Improve breaks into three distinct parts. You need to come up with your possible solutions, select the most appropriate and make sure they will work!

Ideally, you will have conducted a Tollgate Review at the end of each of these steps.

In Step 4, Generate possible solutions, it may be more a case of building on some of the things you have done already in the Measure and Analyse phases. Process stapling and Value-Add Analysis may well have provided clear indicators towards the potential solution, but care is always needed to avoid going down the wrong track.

That can be especially true if the Pilot undertaken in Step 6 is not run appropriately. Use it to genuinely satisfy yourself that the solution will work and to test out your Implementation Plan that will be needed in the final Control phase.

And remember the importance of the handover process – don't let all your hard work be wasted by not getting this element properly agreed.

Before you move into the Control phase, you will need to review the customer and business benefits to really satisfy yourselves that the approach will achieve the goals set.

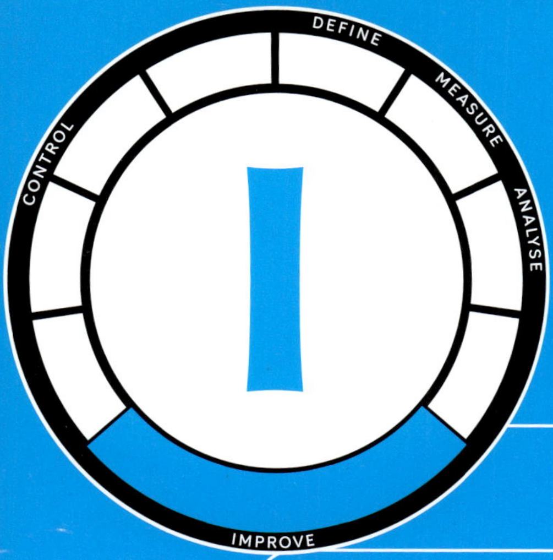

- Generate possible solutions
- Test them where feasible
- Prioritise and select solution(s)
- Review the Stakeholder Analysis
- Pilot the solution(s)
- Refine the solution(s) as necessary
- Build in prevention, where appropriate
- Finalise the Implementation Plan
- Update the Improvement Charter, Storyboard and Communications Plan

Review – Confirm the customer and business benefits

What's this step all about?

The second of the Benefit Reviews looks to confirm the deliverables from the project, and secure authority for the solution to be fully implemented.

As with Quantify the Opportunity, the review also provides an opportunity to look at the project more generally, and key questions will include:

- How are things going?
- Are we on course?
- What have we learnt? And forgotten?
- What's gone well, and why?
- Can the solution be applied elsewhere?
- What conclusions can be drawn?

The main focus, though, is to confirm the deliverables. In completing the Improve phase, you should feel confident that the chosen solution will address the root cause, and ensure you meet the project goals.

Given that management by fact is a key principle of Lean Six Sigma, you should have appropriate measurement data and evidence from the Pilot that your solution will deliver.

There could be quite a range of differing benefits including, for example:

- Reduced errors and waste
- Faster cycle time
- Improved customer satisfaction
- Reduced cost

In assessing how well these match the project objectives, do remember that it may be difficult to quantify the softer benefits of enhanced customer satisfaction. And in projecting when the benefits are likely to emerge, don't lose sight of the fact that there will most probably be a time gap between the cause and effect, especially where customer perception data is concerned.

Apart from looking at the benefits, this review also looks to confirm any costs associated with the solution and its implementation. Again, your Piloting activity should have helped you pull this information together, provided you have treated it as though it were a full-scale implementation.

It's likely there will be internal guidelines to help you assess and present the benefits and costs, but either way, do make sure you have documented the assumptions behind your benefits assessment.

Key outputs from this step

- Confirmation the project is on track
- Confidence in the solution and implementation plan
- A confirmed benefit analysis complete with documented assumptions
- Updated Improvement Charter

Key questions before moving on

- Are we confident that our benefit statement can be justified?
- Have we documented our assumptions?
- Do we feel that expenses associated with implementing the required changes can now be reliably forecast and controlled?
- Given the lessons from our Pilot, do we need to review our team membership for the final implementation?

Step 7 – Implement, standardise and control

What's this step all about?

After all your hard work, you need to implement the solution in a way that ensures you make the gain you expected and hold it! If you are to continue your efforts in reducing variation and cutting out waste, then the changes being made to the process need to be consistently deployed and followed. The handover process is vital. In terms of the tools and techniques for this step, there is little that we haven't already covered previously, though we will be introducing the need for a Control Plan.

Getting the right measures in place will be a vital element of that, and you'll need to be satisfied that the Data Collection Plan has been effectively deployed. Your various DMAIC and, where appropriate, DMADV projects help the organisation move towards a situation where processes are genuinely managed and meet the objectives set out below:

- The process is owned
- There's a clear customer focused objective with prioritised CTQs
- There's a Process Map at the different levels
- There's a well-managed Data Collection Process
- There's a balance of input, in-process and output measures
- It's in an ideal state, or there is an improvement plan in place to move it to that status
- It has been error-proofed
- There's a response plan

If the project has been conducted correctly, and followed the roadmap, then you should be able to tick these various elements as being in place. Several of these are key ingredients of a Control Plan.

The key outputs

- The solution has been implemented and the revised process deployed in a standard way
- Documentation has been updated
- Training has been deployed
- The ongoing Data Collection Plan is in place
- Statistical data demonstrating that the process is 'in control'; though remember that initially your Control Chart may show a special cause evidencing the improvement has worked. So, for example, where you were looking to reduce cycle time, the evidence may be seven points in a row below the mean, enabling you to recalculate the control limits once you have a little more data
- Confirmation of an effective handover
- An updated Storyboard
- An updated Communications Plan

Key questions before moving on

- Following any adjustments from the Pilot, what is the new standard method, process, product or service?
- How have the changes to the process documentation been standardised?
- Are there any implications for internal or external audit?
- Have all the people who do this work been trained?
- How will the measures we've put in place help us monitor ongoing results and prompt further improvement actions?
- Has the handover process worked so that roles and responsibilities are clear?

Key tools for this step

The Control Plan and Process Management Chart

The Control Plan looks to ensure that the gains are achieved from your improved process, and are held. It also provides the framework to prompt further improvement activity.

It can take a variety of formats, but ideally incorporates three main elements:

- The first column captures the Deployment Flow-chart
- The middle column identifies the checks and measures in the process that help you monitor quality and performance
- The third column identifies the actions that need to be taken depending upon what the measures are showing. In part, this links to the Response Plan

Process	Performance	Action
Deployment Flowchart	Checks and Measures	Corrective Actions
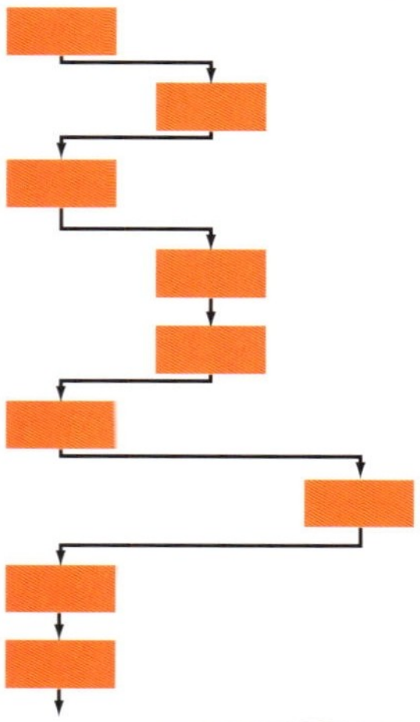	Plot time on each step; should be two hours or less; check for special causes Count errors	If time exceeds two hours, alert team leader and organise investigation If more than one per order, stop process, contact team leader and investigate

If we have completed the Measure and Analyse phase correctly, it should be relatively straightforward to determine the ongoing balance of measures. In monitoring the process, you will need to compare the current and past performance to help ensure that you have secured the intended improvement. And you will need to be able to predict future performance, too, in order to identify the opportunity for further improvement:

Monitoring a process

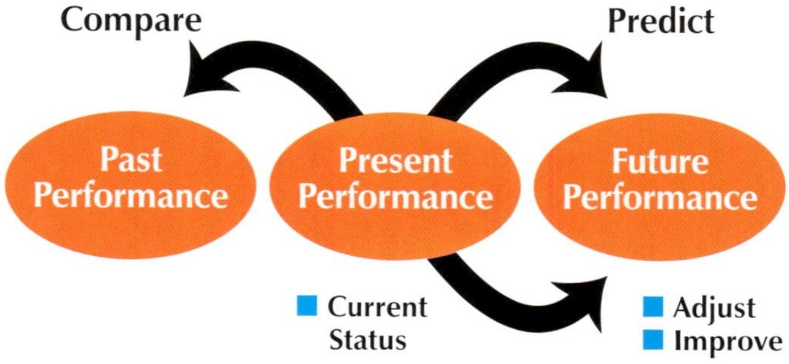

As you can see, there is a clear link to the Response Plan.

Response Plan

In order to manage processes effectively, you need a number of things in place, including:

- A clear customer focused objective with prioritised customer requirements (the CTQs)
- A Process Map
- A balance of input, in-process and output measures
- A Response Plan

A Response Plan highlights the actions to take when something goes wrong. This might cover anything from the identification of a special cause, to the receipt of a customer complaint, to a major systems failure, for example.

Almost certainly, you will have a disaster recovery plan for the organisation that provides a clear summary of what has to be done and by whom. The Response Plan ensures that at a process level everyone understands what has to be done, and by whom, in the event of certain situations.
Use Kipling's Serving Men as a checklist for the actions.

The use of Jidoka, FMEA, and PDPC, the prevention tools, and Negative Brainstorming can help develop an appropriate plan. The format of PDPC provides an ideal framework for the Response Plan.

Overall Process Effectiveness

As we indicated earlier, there are a number of 'Lean Thinking' measures that could have been introduced in the Measure or Analyse phase. These included Takt time that we covered in Quantify the Opportunity on page 94.

Another option, and one that might be helpful as an ongoing measure to monitor overall performance is OEE or OPE.

In manufacturing we use Overall Equipment Effectiveness (OEE); in transactional processes, we refer to Overall Process Effectiveness (OPE).

There's always 'ope

Either way, it's used to measure and understand the performance and effectiveness of equipment or processes, and takes three elements:

- The availability rate measures downtime losses from equipment failures and adjustments as a percentage of scheduled time
- The performance rate measures operating speed losses – running at speeds lower than design speed and stoppages lasting seconds
- The quality rate expresses losses due to scrap and rework as a percentage of total parts run

These elements are multiplied together as shown in this example:

- OEE = Availability x Performance x Quality
    - With Availability at 90%
    - Performance at 95%
    - Quality at 99%
- OEE = .90 X .95 X .99 = 84.6%

In service organisations, or for transactional processes, Overall Process Effectiveness (OPE) may be a better fit. Here you take the following three elements, again multiplying them together to determine the OPE:

- A = availability of equipment
- P = productivity
- Q = quality rate

Let's look at an example, where the Order Input time has a 'theoretical unit time' of 1.5 minutes. The newly installed system has been experiencing some launch problems and therefore is not always on-line when it's needed. On average, it is down 90 minutes every day out of a working day of 7 hours.

We process 200 units in the day; but in addition, we are still getting 15% re-inputting throughout the day. So, what is the OPE?

Let's start with the Availability calculation:

$$\text{Availability} = \frac{\text{Available time} - \text{Down time}}{\text{Available time}} \times 100$$

$$\text{Availability} = \frac{420 \text{ minutes} - 90 \text{ minutes}}{420 \text{ minutes}} \times 100 = 79\%$$

With the Productivity calculation, the formula is:

$$\text{Productivity} = \frac{\text{Unit time x units processed}}{\text{Productive time}} \times 100$$

$$\text{Productivity} = \frac{1.5 \times 200}{330 \text{ minutes}} \times 100 = 91\%$$

And for the Quality calculation, the formula is:

$$\text{Quality} = \frac{\text{Units processed} - \text{number of defective units}}{\text{Units processed}} \times 100$$

$$\text{Quality} = \frac{200 - 30}{200} \times 100 = 85\%$$

What's your Overall Process Effectiveness?

So, the OPE calculation becomes:

Availability x Productivity x Quality

0.79 x 0.91 x 0.85 = 61.1%

Process Review Meetings and Visual Management

The secret's out!

These meetings are one of the secret ingredients for success. The key is holding them regularly to review and maintain performance. But keep them focused and keep them short. Ideally, they are complemented with Visual Management. Here, the workplace has a variety of displays, charts, signs, labels, colour-coded markings, and so on. This helps everyone see what is going on, understand the process, and know what is being done correctly. A key benefit of the 'visual workplace' is that it helps show if something is out of place or missing. Displays and controls could include data or information to the people in the area, keeping them informed on overall performance, or focused on specific quality issues. Visual controls could also cover safety, production throughput, material flow, or quality metrics, for example.

See what I mean?

Monitoring a process helps answer a number of key questions, including:

- What is the current performance level?
- Has the performance changed?
    - In terms of inputs?
    - In terms of in-process activity?
- Do we need to take action with our suppliers?
- Do we need to improve or adjust the process?
- How will the process perform in the future?

One of the secret ingredients for success

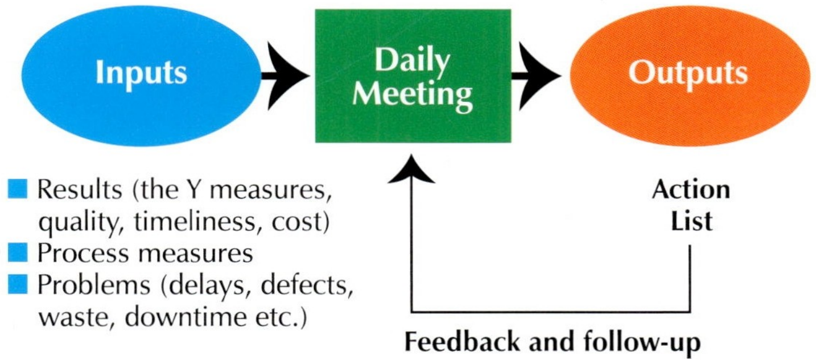

These meetings also provide an opportunity to check that the process is being performed in a consistent and standard way – today's best practice, with all the staff performing the same tasks in the same way.

Remember Pemme…

Once the best way of running the process has been established, you should have an optimum layout of people, equipment and machines that facilitates flow through the process. But in a culture of continuous improvement, further enhancements will be identified.

It's key that the people in the process feel able and are able to put their improvement ideas forward, and that their proposals will be assessed and actioned with the minimum of delay and bureaucracy. If this isn't the case, there is a danger that people will begin to make their own changes to the way the work is carried out and before you know it, variation will have increased and a standard approach will no longer be followed.

Step 8 – Assess achievements and lessons

What's this step all about?

Step 8 is effectively a review for the team. This is where you take stock of the journey and prepare to formally update the Steering Committee, where appropriate.

You will need to consider the following questions:

- Has the 'handover' proved effective?
- Has the process been effectively adopted and deployed?
- Did we solve the problem?
- Are there any symptoms left?
- How well did our plan work?
- What did we learn from this project?
  It's essential the team has learnt from the experience
- It's essential, too, that you can help apply this learning across the organisation

And you will need to determine the accuracy of your earlier benefit analysis, though it may take a while for the change to have an effect. This is also a good time to consider Benchmarking. You understand your process really well; you understand your customer's requirements. There may be clues in other organisations that can help you improve performance further and these will be easier to spot with your improved knowledge. Techniques like the Glyph Diagram provide a good way of capturing Performance Benchmarking Data.

The key outputs

A Storyboard highlighting the key elements.

Key lessons.

Recommendations or ideas about further improvement opportunities.

Evidence of success including actual costs and benefits or at the very least an estimate of when these will be available.

Key questions before moving on to your next project

- How well do the results match our expectations?
- Has the customer noticed? How do we know?
- Given the importance of getting the benefits and financials as accurate as possible, what lessons can we draw for future projects about how we quantified the opportunity, and confirmed the cost benefit analysis?
- Were there any unforeseen effects of the change, and what is their impact?

- How can the solution be improved?
- Have we identified opportunities for prevention?

In assessing how well the results of your improvement activity match the expectations, you might use the Capability Indices to measure the progress made. It could well be that you used this measure as part of the activity undertaken in Step 2 to understand the current situation and provide a baseline position. You'll also find Process Stapling is a good way of checking whether the new process has been deployed effectively.

Did you get what you thought you'd get?

The Glyph

The Glyph is sometimes known as a spider or radar chart. It's a very effective format for presenting a lot of data clearly on one diagram.

What's on your radar?

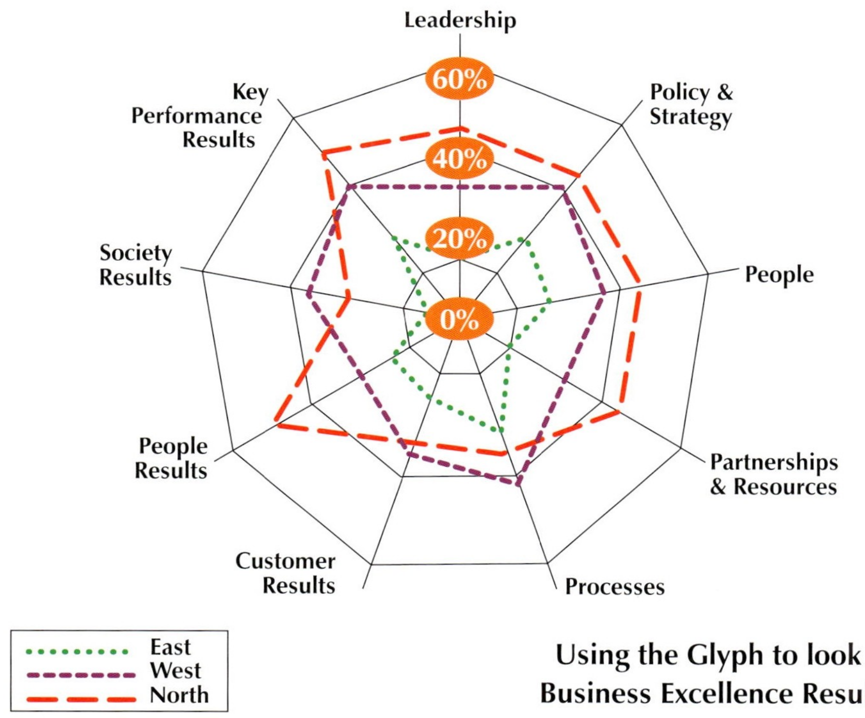

Using the Glyph to look at Business Excellence Results

The diagram shows how it can be used to present the results from an EFQM Business Excellence self-assessment exercise between three different regions of an organisation. It could also show, for example, the results over several years, or perhaps in a similar way, customer or employee survey results.

It's a very good way of presenting Benchmarking data, enabling comparison between different organisations. And now might be a very good time to undertake a Benchmarking Study to prompt further improvement.

Control – a quick summary

So, the solution is in place, the ongoing Control Plan and measures are in place, and all is hunky-dory. Well, let's hope so; it's all too easy to ignore the importance of this phase.

You need to make sure the solution has been appropriately and effectively deployed, and that the relevant people know what's happening and why. Handover responsibilities should be clearly understood to avoid things slipping down the cracks, and a RACI Matrix will help you here.

The organisation's various DMAIC projects help you move towards a situation where processes are genuinely managed and meet the objectives set out below:

- The process is owned
- There's a clear customer focused objective with prioritised customer requirements (the CTQs)
- There's a Process Map at the different levels
- There's a well-managed Data Collection Process
- There's a balance of input, in-process and output measures
- It's in an ideal state, or there is an improvement plan in place to move it to that status
- It has been error-proofed
- There's a response plan

The Benefits Review that follows will help confirm your achievements and identify the key lessons that can be shared both within the team and across the wider organisation.

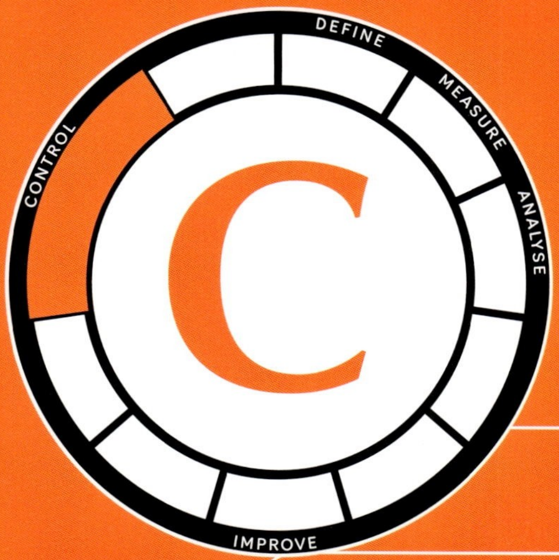

- Implement the solution
- Update documentation
- Carry out training
- Ensure the Handover Plan is followed
- Implement a Control Plan
- Review the project and determine the benefits
- Complete the Improvement Charter, Storyboard and Communications Plan
- Recognise people's contributions and efforts

Final review

What's this step all about?

This is the 'formal' post implementation review involving the project Champion and Steering Committee. It may well involve your team presenting their Storyboard.

The issues in this final review are very similar to those in Step 8, but the Steering Committee should be taking a wider 'business perspective'. Certainly they will be interested to know the real costs and benefits and whether there have been any unexpected debits or credits.

If 'Process Management' is in its early stages of development, the Steering Committee may be particularly interested in how relevant lessons can be applied to progress the approach organisation-wide.

The Champion will need to determine the next steps, if any, for you and your team.

The Champion or Steering Committee should also remember the importance of recognition – almost certainly the team will have worked very hard in tackling this project. At the very least, a personal 'thank-you' will be appropriate.

Key questions to expect from the Steering Committee

How satisfied are you that the problem has been solved?

What is the new Process Sigma performance? What was the baseline figure?

What benefits have been realised or are in the pipeline?

How accurate was the cost benefit analysis?

Do our customers feel there has been an improvement? How do you know?

Are there lessons, ideas or 'best practices' that can be applied elsewhere in the business?

What should happen to this team now?

What should we do to suitably recognise the team's success and efforts?

The Champions...

Follow me – I'm right behind you

Improvement teams need the support, commitment, and availability of a Project Champion. These are the people who will get behind your initiatives to deliver better customer experiences.

Champions have a number of key responsibilities. In addition to selecting the project and the improvement team, they need to:

- Provide strategic direction for the project team
- Develop and agree the Improvement Charter ensuring the scope is stretching but manageable
- Keep themselves informed on the project's progress and take an active role in the Tollgates and Reviews
- Help the team overcome roadblocks
- Facilitate the identification of resources for the team as needed
- Keep the team focused on the desired results – there will be plenty of tempting detours
- Keep management and the organisation appropriately informed
- Spread the message
- Identify future improvement team leaders
- Ensure appropriate reward and recognition
- Provide budget/resources
- Be prepared to stop the project
- Look for new projects (sub-projects)

Avoid the M1 and M25!

Don't forget the elephant!

Projects are more likely to be successful if they relate to key business issues. People will realise the project is important and will understand the benefits. But remember to eat the elephant in bite-size chunks!

Teams are successful when they know what to do, why it's being done and how to do it. And as we indicated previously, they'll need to know they have the Champion's support and respect. Champions need to be flexible in the way they work with their team, to help them accomplish their goals.

Some of the challenges they are likely to face are summarised on the following page.

10 challenges facing Champions

Generating a list of the challenges facing Champions and their teams is easy!

Remember Hercules?

The list below reflects many of the common problems experienced in organisations. You might want to generate your own list using Negative Brainstorming. It's good fun, albeit somewhat daunting when you consider the output.

1. Ineffective Improvement Charters that are, for example, too vague or too large.
2. Team members don't always share a unified direction or vision.

Share the vision

3. The wrong mix of skills or functional representation in the team.
4. Champions, team members or leaders not spending enough time on the projects.
5. Pressure for immediate financial impact leads to inappropriate shortcuts that frustrate the team members and discredit the systematic approach being promoted.
6. Other key stakeholders are not fully supportive of the project or the team's approach.
7. Inadequate budget to complete the project or implement recommended solutions.
8. Competing or conflicting project objectives among different improvement teams simply lead to confusion.
9. 'Scope creep' – the project keeps getting bigger.

Watch out for that big creep!

10. Poorly managed handovers, that fail to integrate the improvements into the organisation.

The important thing is to be aware of these issues and actively seek to anticipate and prevent them.

The Lean Six Sigma Improvement Journey Tools and Techniques

As you can see from this table, the Quality Improvement Tools and Techniques can be applied in a very flexible way. I'm sure you will find other ways of using them! But use them in a way which helps you.

	D	M	A	I			C	
▼ Tool	Step 1	Step 2	Step 3	Step 4	Step 5	Step 6	Step 7	Step 8
Affinity Diagram	✓	✓	✓			✓	✓	
Arrow Diagram						✓	✓	
Ask Why		✓	✓					
Backwards Visioning	✓						✓	
Benchmarking	✓	✓						✓
Brainstorming	✓		✓	✓				
Capability		✓	✓			✓	✓	✓
CATALYST				✓				
Cell Manufacturing		✓		✓				
Control Charts	✓	✓				✓	✓	✓
Control Plan							✓	
CTQs	✓	✓				✓	✓	
Data Collection	✓	✓	✓	✓	✓	✓	✓	✓
Deployment Flow-chart		✓	✓	✓			✓	
Design of Experiments		✓	✓	✓				
Drum Buffer Rope		✓	✓	✓			✓	
Elevator Speech	✓				✓	✓		
Ergonomics			✓	✓				
Error Proofing				✓		✓		
Fifteen Word Flipchart	✓				✓	✓		
Fishbone			✓	✓				
Five Ss				✓			✓	
FMEA	✓		✓			✓	✓	
Force Field Diagram	✓				✓	✓		
Glyph		✓						✓
Grip	✓	✓	✓	✓	✓	✓	✓	
Heijunka		✓	✓	✓			✓	
Hypothesis Testing			✓			✓	✓	
Idea Box				✓				
Improvement Charter	✓	✓	✓		✓			✓
In Frame/Out of Frame	✓		✓					
Interrelationship Diagram	✓		✓			✓	✓	
Is/Is Not	✓		✓					
Jidoka	✓		✓	✓		✓	✓	
Just in Time		✓		✓				
Kanban				✓				
▲ Tool	Step 1	Step 2	Step 3	Step 4	Step 5	Step 6	Step 7	Step 8
	D	M	A	I			C	

	D	M	A	I			C	
▼ **Tool**	**Step 1**	**Step 2**	**Step 3**	**Step 4**	**Step 5**	**Step 6**	**Step 7**	**Step 8**
Matrix Diagram	✓	✓	✓		✓	✓	✓	
Measurement	✓	✓	✓	✓	✓	✓	✓	✓
Moments of Truth		✓	✓					
Multi-Generation Plan	✓		✓					✓
N/3	✓		✓		✓			
Negative Brainstorming			✓	✓		✓		
Overall Process Effectiveness		✓	✓				✓	
Paired Comparisons	✓		✓		✓			
Pareto	✓	✓	✓		✓			
Piloting				✓		✓		
Priority Based Matrix	✓		✓		✓			
Process Sigma		✓	✓			✓	✓	✓
Process Stapling		✓	✓	✓			✓	✓
PDPC	✓		✓			✓	✓	✓
Pull Production		✓	✓	✓				
RACI	✓					✓	✓	
Random Words				✓				
Response Plan							✓	
Sampling		✓	✓					
Scatter Diagram			✓	✓				
Seven Wastes		✓	✓					
Single Piece Flow		✓		✓				
SMED			✓	✓				
Spaghetti Diagram		✓	✓	✓				
Stakeholder Analysis	✓				✓	✓		
Storyboard	✓	✓	✓	✓	✓	✓	✓	✓
SIPOC	✓	✓		✓			✓	
Takt Time	✓	✓	✓	✓	✓	✓	✓	✓
Theory of Constraints		✓	✓	✓			✓	
Thinking Hats	✓			✓				
Three Ds Matrix	✓				✓	✓		
Tree Diagram	✓		✓			✓	✓	
Value-Add		✓	✓			✓	✓	
Value Stream Map		✓	✓	✓			✓	
Visual Management							✓	
XY Grid	✓				✓	✓		
▲ **Tool**	**Step 1**	**Step 2**	**Step 3**	**Step 4**	**Step 5**	**Step 6**	**Step 7**	**Step 8**
	D	M	A	I			C	

Where to use the tools

I need to clarify the improvement project

- Improvement Charter
- Affinity Diagram
- Interrelationship Diagram
- Thinking Hats
- In Frame Out Of Frame
- Fifteen Word Flipchart
- Grip
- RACI
- Is/Is Not
- Multi-Generation Plan

I need to gain support and influence the stakeholders

- Force Field Diagram
- Stakeholder Analysis
- XY Grid
- Elevator Speech
- Three Ds Matrix
- Backwards Visioning

I need to understand the Voice of the Customer

- CTQs
- Moments of Truth
- Affinity Diagram
- Tree Diagram
- Paired Comparisons

I need to understand how the process works

- SIPOC
- Process Stapling
- Deployment Flow-chart
- Value Add Analysis
- Spaghetti Diagram
- Ask Why
- Value Stream Mapping
- Theory of Constraints
- Just in Time

I need to improve the process flow

- Theory of Constraints
- Drum Buffer Rope
- Cell Manufacturing
- Product Families
- Pull Production/Kanban
- Just in Time
- Heijunka
- Five Ss

I need to quantify a problem or situation

- Measurement
- Data Collection
- Sampling
- Control Charts
- Process Sigma
- Process Capability
- Takt Time
- Overall Process Effectiveness
- Seven Wastes

I need to analyse and present data

- Control Charts/Capability
- Pareto Analysis
- Scatter Diagram
- XY Grids
- The Glyph
- Hypothesis Testing
- Design of Experiments
- Takt Time
- Seven Wastes
- Value-Add Analysis
- Overall Process Effectiveness

I need to generate/group ideas

- Brainstorming (Negative)
- Affinity Diagram
- Thinking Hats
- Catalyst
- Idea Box
- Random Words
- Fishbone Diagram
- Ask Why

I need to understand the connections between ideas or issues

- Interrelationship Diagram
- Scatter Diagram
- Matrix Diagram
- Design of Experiments

I need to understand the pros and cons of a situation

- Force Field Diagram
- Stakeholder Analysis
- Thinking Hats

I need to make decisions or determine the priorities or sequence for action

- Paired Comparisons & N/3
- Priority Based Matrix
- Pareto Analysis
- XY Grids
- Force Field Diagram
- Interrelationship Diagram
- Tree Diagram
- Arrow Diagram
- Multi-Generation Plan

I need to ensure the effective implementation of our solution

- Piloting
- PDPC
- FMEA/Error Proofing
- Brainstorming (Negative)
- Tree Diagram
- Arrow Diagram
- RACI Responsibility Matrix
- Control Plan
- Response Plan

I need to prevent problems or make contingencies

- Jidoka
- FMEA
- PDPC
- Error Proofing
- Brainstorming (Negative)
- Control Plan
- Response Plan
- Process Review Meetings
- Visual Management

I need to standardise things as far as possible

- Control Plan
- SIPOC
- Process Stapling
- Flow-Chart
- Data Collection
- Five Ss
- Heijunka
- Process Review Meetings
- Visual Management

Affinity Diagram: 10-11, 20
Arrow Diagram: 117-118
Ask Why: 80
Autonomation: 101
Backwards Visioning: 29
Batches: 102
Benchmarking: 133
Brainstorming: 76-77, 96
Bottlenecks: *see Theory of Constraints*
Capability: 66-67
Catalyst: 106
Cell Manufacturing: 103
Champions: 138-139
Check Sheet: 53, 76
Concentration Diagram: 53
Constraints: *see Theory of Constraints*
Control Charts (SPC): 4, 60-65, 84
Control Plan: 128
Creative Tools and Techniques: 105-107
CTQs: 2, 3, 20, 115
Data Collection: 50-54
Defects Per Million Opportunities: 68-69
Deployment Flow-chart: 41-42, 104
Design of Experiments: 86-89
DMADV: 4
Drum Buffer Rope: 104
Elevator Speech: 30
Error Proofing: 120-121
Ergonomics: 98
Failure Modes and Effects Analysis: *see FMEA*
Fifteen Word Flipchart: 16, 30
Fishbone Diagram: 11, 79, 96
Five Ss: 97-98
Five Whys: *see Ask Why*
Flow-charts: 40-43
FMEA: 119-120
Force Field Diagram: 27
Gauge R&R: 52
Gemba: 3
Glyph Diagram: 133
GRIP: 31-32
Handover: 121
Heijunka: 100
Hypothesis Testing: 84-86
Idea Box: 107
Implementation Plan: 121
Improvement Charter: 12-15
In Frame/Out of Frame: 16
Input and In-process Measures: 49, 54
Interrelationship Diagram: 11, 80-81
Is/Is Not: 78
Jidoka: 101
Just in Time: 101
Kaizen Rapid Improvement Event: 107
Kanban: 102
Levelling: *see Heijunka*
Managing Change: 5
Matrix Diagram: 20, 50, 54, 110, 115
Measurement: 48-49
Moments of Truth: 42, 47
Muda: *see Waste*
Multi-Generation Plan: 95
N/3: 109
Negative Brainstorming: 76-77, 96, 105, 120
Operational Definition: 52
Output Measures: 48, 50
Overall Process Effectiveness: 129-130
Paired Comparisons: 109
Pareto Analysis: 75, 76
Piloting: 114
PONC: 75
Priority Based Matrix: 110
Process Capability Index (Cp, Cpk): 66-67
Process Decision Programme Chart: 33, 119
Process Management: 126, 134
Process Maps: 40-43